Psalms Alive! is a great springboard for discussion in a group. David presents the Scripture, shows how it applies to his life, and then leaves you with some questions to challenge you—and in my case my brothers—to further dig into the Word he has presented. This book will be a great resource to help us further in our walk and lead us into engaging discussions as well. Thanks David!

Andrew Nicholls, Men's Bible Study Leader, Ottawa, ON

David writes not as if using pen and ink, but as if he was actually in the room with the reader having a fireside chat over a cup of coffee (or tea if you prefer). The practical applications and the questions to ponder at the end of each study give the reader a time to reflect on what he has read and a time to "be still" for a few moments to listen for the voice of God to speak and minister to his heart. As David put it so well in the Epilogue of this book, "I meet with God in the Psalms," I too met with God as I read the various Psalms in *Psalms Alive!* and it was a meeting well worth my time.

Garry Cline, Praise & Worship Leader,
N. Manchester Missionary Church, N. Manchester, IN

No matter how many times you've read the Psalms, David Kitz's dramatic rendering is sure to bring new revelation and insight. You'll smile at the mirth around the family table, stand in awe under a canopy of stars, then weep at a tsunami's destructive power, and through it all see the wonder and working of God. It is my fervent hope that everyone reads this book!

Keith Clemons
Award winning author of Angel in the Alley

Psalms Alive! is Canadian! Yes, what a delight to have a meditational study that is biblically sound and makes you cry and belly laugh at the same time. Author David Kitz has done it again and has brought the truth of the Psalms to life.

Rev. Karen Middleton, Tent of David, Rockland, ON

As a person living with hereditary vision impairment, I am highly auditory. David Kitz has such a way of dramatizing the Psalms in word and vocal inflection that I find myself immediately drawn into and captivated by the scene before me. My imagination and emotions are actively participating in every situation. Whether through recorded media, live performance, or personal interaction, the life of Christ radiates through David.

Rose Misner, co-pastor, Amazing Love Fellowship, Saint John, NB

The Psalms are like the waves of the sea. They express the high ups and low downs of human emotions, from upmost praise and joy to depths of fear, anger, and sadness. Although the waters rage and strong winds blow, David Kitz captains his readers through both still and stormy seas with skill, insight, and wit. *Psalms Alive!* is as instructive as it is delightful to read.

Dr. Barry Buzza, president, Foursquare Gospel Church of Canada

As I read *Psalms Alive!* something remarkable happened. The Psalms literally began to come alive to me. It is as if the writings with the insights then become interactive as we relate to biblical David and his particular reason for writing each Psalm. We are able to sense and experience what he must have been thinking as he penned these words, which then became part of the Holy Scriptures.

Doug Sprunt, Salem Storehouse, Ottawa, ON

As a pastor I'm always looking for helpful, usable, and understandable resources to assist me with the task of sharing God's Word with His people. David Kitz has provided just such a resource in *Psalms Alive!* By weaving personal experience, current events, and down to earth illustrations into his reflections on each Psalm, David helps lead the reader into a deeper understanding of the Psalms and their relevance to daily life. This is a very creative, practical, and useful tool for any study or discussion of the Psalms.

Rev. Daryl Solie
Pastor, Prince of Peace Lutheran Church, Regina, SK

What gives a book credence? The credibility of its author. So as a friend and weekly companion in a men's group, let me comment briefly on David Kitz, the man.

He is the real deal. He loves life. He cares about people. He's tender but courageous. He takes on big challenges. Having faced his share of hardships, he keeps bouncing back by fixing his gaze upward. Most of all, he loves God passionately. In fact, he reminds me of the other David he loves to study and write about—King David! So for all these reasons, I recommend you read this book.

Lyle Johnson
Next Level Ministries

Psalms Alive!

Blake,

May the Psalms come alive for you as never before!

David Kitz

psalms alive!
connecting heaven and earth

DAVID KITZ

forever books
WINNIPEG CANADA
www.foreverbooks.ca

Forever Books

WINNIPEG CANADA
www.foreverbooks.ca

Dedication

To my wife,
Karen Kitz,
whose patience I may try,
but whose love I enjoy.

Acknowledgments

A NUMBER OF YEARS AGO, I spent a pivotal evening in a darkened auditorium watching the Gospel of Luke come alive before my eyes. A one-man biblical drama had me totally absorbed. As the actor, Bruce Kuhn, held me in his magical spell, I sensed the Holy Spirit whisper, "This is what I want you to do with the Psalms."

To my surprise that pivotal evening became the first of many steps that would ultimately lead to you holding this book in your hands. Of course a great deal has happened in the interim. In addition to the spark that Bruce Kuhn ignited that evening, I have a number of people I should thank for their help along the way.

As I began my own one-man dramatizations of the Psalms, Wilf Wight of the Canadian Bible Society played a significant role in arranging events and giving me much-needed encouragement. He saw immeasurable worth in bringing God's Word to life in this rather unconventional way. Without his help in those early stages, I am not sure if I would have persevered.

After several years of memorizing, dramatizing, and reflecting upon the Psalms, I felt prompted to write about the transformational power of these selected Psalms and their impact on my life. A number of people have been a help and encouragement in the writing process, but none more so than Tim Peterson, the past president of the Foursquare Gospel Church of Canada (1992–2007). Tim has such a gentle way of nudging me closer to the Source of the Psalms. I could call Tim Peterson my proofreader, but in reality he was more my proof-thinker—keeping me true to the meaning, spirit, and intent of each Psalm. Thanks, Tim.

For believers, all too often our walk of faith turns into the slacker's coast. We coast on the faith of others—our spouse, our pastor, a godly parent, or a faithful friend. The slacker's coast has been part of my experience too. But in the last few years, I have been blessed to find myself in a group of Christ's apprentices, who on a weekly basis challenge me to dig deeper and reach higher. Specifically, I want to thank Lyle Johnson and the men of Next Level Ministries. Meeting with a group of dedicated men of like mind each Friday morning has truly taken my walk of faith to the next level. Thanks for encouraging me to heed Christ's call and step out of the boat.[1]

---

[1] *If You Want to Walk on Water, You've Got to Get Out of the Boat* by John Ortberg, Zondervan, copyright 2001.

Contents

Foreword

OVER THE YEARS I HAVE COME to appreciate the diversity of God in new dimensions. The creativity of God is revealed in nature—in the incredible variety of just the color green for instance. While in New Zealand several years ago I wondered, "How did God come up with all the ideas?" That same creative variety is expressed in the unique gifts and talents which we see at work in God's people.

David Kitz is unique. I met David several years ago after reading his award-winning novel, *The Soldier, the Terrorist, and the Donkey King*. I so appreciated the perspective he presented about Jesus.

In *Psalms Alive! Connecting Heaven and Earth*, David opens his heart to let God speak to him through the beautiful songs, meditations, and reflections of the biblical Psalms. As an actor, David helps you visualize the drama of the moment. As a writer, he paints a verbal picture that helps you look back into your own life to see and appreciate what God has done, what He is doing, and also bring faith to your heart for what He can still do in you.

This book has been written to help open your heart to the healing grace of our wonderful God—connecting you to heaven. As you read, expect the Psalms to come alive for you as never before.

Enjoy!

Willard Thiessen, television host of *It's a New Day*

Preface

The Psalms speak to our deepest needs!

God speaks to us—to humanity—through His Word. This has been the case since the first God-inspired, God-directed scribe took pen in hand. For over three millennia men and women have heard the voice of God through words of Holy Scripture.

How do we draw meaning from these words? In the twenty-first century, can the Word of God come alive to us and speak to our hearts? Are there insights we can gain by looking at the prayer and devotional life of the ancient Hebrews?

Within the Psalms we hear the deepest longings of the human heart. Here we find the full range of human experiences—experiences that brings us face to face with God. Our joys and triumphs are reflected here. Our spirits soar to the heavens, but we also plumb the depths of tragedy and despair. Is it any wonder then, that throughout the ages men and women have found refuge in the Psalms?

Of course, the Book of Psalms is only a portion of the Bible and this *"word of God is living and active. Sharper than any double-edged sword, it penetrates even to dividing soul and spirit, joints and marrow; it judges the thoughts and attitudes of the heart"* (Hebrews 4:12).

The above Scripture is the premise on which this book is built. When we handle the Word of God, we are handling life. When we take hold of the Word of God, it takes hold of us. Meditating on God's Word is not a passive activity. These words from God have transformational power built right into them.

You are about to begin interacting with God's Word found in the Book of Psalms. Each chapter in this book follows a similar format. A psalm or a portion of a psalm is presented. This is followed by the author's thoughts on this Scripture portion. Finally, under the heading, *Bringing Life to the Psalms*, there are a series of suggested activities or questions for further consideration. They are suitable for personal reflection or may be used to trigger discussion in small groups.

The purpose throughout this book is to let God's Word speak. The author's thoughts—my thoughts—on the Psalms are, in fact, secondary. They are my way of saying, "God talked to me in this way about this psalm. This is how the truths of this psalm have played out in my life. Now the question becomes, what about you? What is God saying to you through this psalm?"

God wants to bring these same Scriptures alive in the context of your life, in the here and now. The God who inspired the Psalms—who spoke through and to David—wants to speak to and through you as well. That's what this walk with God is all about—two-way communication rooted in relationship, nurtured in prayer and praise, and planted on the rock-solid foundation of the Word of God.

When Jesus was tempted in the wilderness, the devil urged him to turn stones into bread. Jesus responded by saying, *"It is written: 'Man does not live on bread alone, but on every word that comes from the mouth of God'"* (Matthew 4:4).

If, for you, God's Word has been as palatable as stone, then ask the Holy Spirit to bring His Word to life. In the Psalms we find life. We encounter real people—David and the other psalmists—in a real relationship with the living God.

For the past number of years I have been bringing the Psalms to life for audiences through the medium of live drama. Here now in book form, from a dramatist's perspective, I provide a glimpse into the prayers and praise of the psalmists.

As you read, listen. Listen and let God speak. Let Him speak to you heart-to-heart through His living Word. Come now and find yourself before your God, through the eternal poetry of the Psalms.

The First Witness Speaks

A psalm of David

The heavens declare the glory of God;
the skies proclaim the work of his hands.
Day after day they pour forth speech;
night after night they display knowledge.
There is no speech or language where their
voice is not heard.
Their voice goes out into all the earth,
their words to the ends of the world.
In the heavens he has pitched a tent for the sun,
which is like a bridegroom coming forth from
his pavilion,
like a champion rejoicing to run his course.
It rises at one end of the heavens and makes its
circuit to the other;
nothing is hidden from its heat.

WHEN WAS THE LAST TIME YOU
went for a walk beneath a canopy of stars? Now, I'm not talking
about catching a fleeting glimpse of a dozen or so stars obscured by
the incessant glare of city streetlights. I'm talking about walking

beneath a canopy of stars, visible in their myriads, stretching from horizon to horizon. That is a truly awe-inspiring experience!

That is where David begins this psalm. He begins it beneath the stars. He begins it beneath a sky so big it reduces any who behold it to a mere speck of insignificance—a speck below the glorious vastness above. Can you see him standing there, the youthful shepherd on the Judean hillside, gazing into the face of eternity?

And eternity is talking. The sky is talking to him.

What is it saying? Can you hear its words?

David can. He hears it pouring forth speech. And it is not just the night sky that's talking to him. The heavens are speaking continually, day and night. This is an endless conversation heard around the world.

You see, the sky speaks a language understood by all. Who has not stopped and stood in wonder at the sight of a dazzling sunset, marveled at the shafts of light beaming down from behind a thunderhead, been amazed by the appearance of a rainbow, or perhaps you have seen the aurora whirl and dance across the sky?

These experiences are universal. They are available to all, on every continent, in every nation, to every language and people group.

The sky is talking. Are you listening? Do you understand the words?

"I am the Creator. I am the Maker of the heavens and the earth. I am the Author of beauty, the Fount of life, the Giver of knowledge, the ageless One. I am food for the hungry, water of life for the thirsty, wisdom for the seeking soul. I am bigger than your problems, more vast than the oceans, deeper than the abyss, higher than the sky.

I am eternal.

I am here.

I am."

I AM is speaking.

Is He speaking to you?

Theologians call these words spoken from the sky the "testimony of nature." It is considered by many to be one of the primary or foremost arguments for the existence of God. In a court of law, it is essential that witnesses who are called to the stand speak audibly, so their testimony can be heard by all.

In this psalm we hear David's implied question to us, "Have you heard the sky speaking? Do you hear the testimony, the words the heavens are proclaiming to your heart?"

We are all summoned to this cosmic courtroom. All of the humanity is there. We may all listen to the testimony of this witness. Everyone under the sun can hear these words. They are as loud as the blaring brilliance of the sun at high noon, or as soft as the glow of the most distant star.

Are you listening? Can you hear them now—these words that the sky above declares?

Some nine hundred years after David penned Psalm 19, the apostle Paul wrote these words about humankind:

> *What may be known about God is plain to them, because God has made it plain to them. For since the creation of the world God's invisible qualities—his eternal power and divine nature—have been clearly seen, being understood from what has been made, so that men are without excuse (Romans 1:19–20).*

In effect, Paul is saying the sky has been talking all this time. In fact, the entirety of nature has been declaring the power and character of this awesome Creator God. Have you not heard Him in the thundering waterfall, caught a glimpse of His reflection in the azure mountain lake, picked up His whisper beneath the ocean breakers' roar? Have you not heard nature testifying to the grandeur and majesty of the Creator?

Are you deaf or have you chosen not to hear?

Romans chapter one is in fact a ringing indictment against humankind. Beneath the sky that covers us all, we have been summoned. We have come to the court of the universe. Heaven's witnesses have spoken, and they are a multitude beyond number. They have addressed us. And we have stopped our ears. We have refused to listen.

Surely, God's judgment on us will follow.

But here in Psalm 19, we see a man with a different heart—a man whose heart is tuned to God—a man who hears the heavens speaking. This is in fact David's distinguishing characteristic. He is a man after God's own heart.

In 1 Samuel, we see that David was chosen to be king over Israel because of this singular trait. Saul was rejected as king because of his refusal to hear and obey the voice of God. In this one sentence of Scripture spoken by Samuel the prophet, we hear the LORD's indictment against Saul and we also hear the LORD's reason for choosing David to replace him: *"But now your kingdom will not endure; the LORD has sought out a man after his own heart and appointed him leader of his people, because you have not kept the LORD's command"* (1 Samuel 13:14).

Where did David develop that heart that sought after God? Could it be that it all began on a starry night as he stood alone on that Judean hillside—a mere speck below the glorious vastness above?

If we cannot hear God in the silence, will we be able to hear Him at all? Unless we cultivate a listening heart, how can we hope to hear Him in the din of life, amid the hectic charge?

I began this chapter with a question: "When was the last time you went for a walk beneath a canopy of stars?"

I must confess that for me it's been years. You see, I am a city dweller, and though I often go for nighttime walks through the park by my home, even on the clearest night only a few of the brightest stars are visible. We have blocked them out. We have made our own lights. Now if we choose to walk at night, we walk by our own light. That age-old communion between humanity and the night sky has been broken, and we are the poorer for it. Edison's fine invention has robbed me of this opportunity to gaze into the face of eternity.

In 2006, the world's population reached a significant milestone: more than 50 per cent of the earth's people now live in an urban environment. The inhabitants of this increasingly urbanized planet are becoming ever more disconnected from the nightly conversation of the heavens—this conversation of which David wrote so many centuries ago. In fact, a kind of cosmic reversal has taken place. Now the darkened planet beams light up into the night sky. Have you seen the satellite photos of North America at night? They show a constellation of cities twinkling along the eastern and western seaboards. Vast conglomerations of light are camped along the Great Lakes. We have developed our own Milky Way. Astronomers lament this light pollution. They must move their star-gazing equipment to ever more remote locations.

What about the common man or woman, the girl or boy who grows up without engaging in this heavenly conversation—a conversation that was so common, so universal, a century ago? They have lost an opportunity to marvel, to stand in awe beneath the transcendent One. This is no minor loss.

In what have we engaged instead? In what are we caught up? Humanity is caught up in a fascination with gadgetry. Techno-wizardry enthralls us. Computers beckon for our time. Radios blare. Televisions drone on. Advertisers flash their images upon our naked brains. And we sit transfixed—entertained, but rarely enlightened; occupied, but rarely enthralled; impressed only with ourselves, but seldom challenged.

25

This is a world turned in on itself, self-absorbed, playing with its own toys. Its back is turned away from God. The heavens flash their message. The skies call out but no one is listening.

Have we forgotten how to stand in awe?

How can we hear God if we have drowned out the stars and the message they bring? If astronomers are in lamentation, then theologians, the God-seekers on this earth, should be on their knees in sackcloth and ashes.

We have silenced the stars. Within our urban environments, their message has been blocked, drowned out by the light of our own creation. Their testimony to the majesty of God has been nullified. Three billion people can no longer hear this witness on a regular, nightly basis.

Is it any wonder that faith in the all-wise Creator God is in decline? And nowhere is this decline more evident than in urban centers.

In cities, even the view of the daytime sky is obstructed. Broad, open vistas are blocked by buildings. All too often, daylight working hours are spent in windowless buildings. Increasingly, smog hinders our view. The testimony of the sky is impeded.

Nevertheless, David's words in this psalm haunt us. The glory of God remains. We may have sullied the skies, but the skies remain. Our view of the sun may be clouded by pollutants, but the sun remains. Our view of the stars may be dimmed by our own lights, but the stars remain. They sing out His glory.

God remains. The unchanging, unfathomable, ageless Creator remains. His desire to communicate with us remains. His voice has not been silenced. He still beckons us out from our self-obsessed focus to seek after Him, to discover His heart.

On that Judean hillside, among those few sheep, little David found himself. He found himself small beneath the hand of the Almighty God. He discovered his smallness, his insignificance, beneath the all-surpassing vastness of God.

Have you discovered your smallness?

Unless we catch a glimpse of God, we are doomed to walk this planet like self-inflated titans, puffed up large in our own eyes but devoid of all meaning. The world is filled with men who strut about in this fashion. King Saul had become such a man, so God sought a man after His own heart. In David he found the right heart—a heart that had been touched by the greatness of God, not the greatness of self. If there is a theme throughout the Psalms, surely this is it. The Psalms are all about the greatness of God.

In a few short weeks, I hope to return to my childhood home. There on the prairies, unobstructed by city lights, I can behold the same stars David saw nearly three thousand years ago. They can begin their magical chant. Again I will hear the words they proclaimed to me as a young farm boy so many years ago. Perhaps they are the same words David heard. They dare not speak of themselves. They speak only of the Source of all light.

Can you hear them?

"I am the Creator. I am the Maker of the heavens and the earth. I am the Author of beauty, the Fount of life, the Giver of knowledge, the ageless One. I am food for the hungry, water of life for the thirsty, wisdom for the seeking soul. I am bigger than your problems, more vast than the oceans, deeper than the abyss, higher than the sky.

I am eternal.

I am here.

I am."

I AM is speaking.

Is He speaking to you?

Bringing Life to the Psalms

1. Plan a personal evening beneath the stars outside the city. Make it a time of listening for God's voice.

2. Have you encountered God in nature? Take a few moments to reflect on that experience. How did you respond as you sensed His presence?

3. Take a daily nature break. Even five minutes spent in a park or garden can rejuvenate the human spirit and bring us more in tune with God.

4. Take time to be alone. Turn off the noise box and listen. Heed the psalmist's admonition, *"Be still, and know that I am God"* (Psalm 46:10). Without a doubt, the Maker of the universe is still speaking. He longs to speak to you.

5. Religious surveys indicate there is a high percentage of atheists and agnostics in the faculties of most secular universities. However, astronomy departments are largely peopled by men and women who have faith in God. How do you account for this discrepancy?

The Second Witness Speaks

The law of the LORD is perfect,
reviving the soul.
The statutes of the Lord are trustworthy,
making wise the simple.
The precepts of the LORD are right,
giving joy to the heart.
The commands of the LORD are radiant,
giving light to the eyes.
The fear of the Lord is pure,
enduring forever.
The ordinances of the LORD are sure
and altogether righteous.
They are more precious than gold,
than much pure gold;
They are sweeter than honey,
than honey from the comb.
By them is your servant warned;
In keeping them there is great reward.

IF NATURE IS THE FIRST WITNESS to testify to the glory of God, then the Scriptures—the written Word of God—constitute the second great witness to speak of God's existence. Both these great witnesses have gathered here to testify within the context of this psalm. The voice of the speaking stars is now joined by the voice of the written Holy Word.

Nowhere else in Scripture are these two witnesses so clearly juxtaposed. They have joined forces—linked arms—to deliver a message to David. And through David they deliver their message to us.

And what is that message? It is a message about the character of God. While nature speaks to us of the existence of God the Creator, it is largely silent regarding the nature or character of this all-powerful supernatural being. Is He good? Is He evil? Is He indifferent to us? Is He angry with us? What is this great, overarching, omnipresent God really like? May we approach Him?

The Scriptures provide us with the answers to these questions. The apostle Peter tells us something of how the Scriptures came into being. He says that *"men spoke from God as they were carried along by the Holy Spirit"* (2 Peter 1:21).

Furthermore, Paul the apostle informed Timothy, his son in the faith, that, *"All Scripture is God-breathed and is useful for teaching, rebuking, correcting and training in righteousness, so that the man of God may be thoroughly equipped for every good work"* (2 Timothy 3:16–17).

What does this second witness, the witness of the Word, testify to David concerning himself and the God of the heavens?

"The law of the LORD is perfect, reviving the soul."

The law is perfect, flawless, inerrant, and infallible. Only a perfect, flawless, inerrant, and infallible God can be the source of such a document. The law of the LORD referred to here is in fact the Bible, the Word of God. Jack Hayford, in his commentary on this verse from the Psalms[2], states, "That the *'law of the LORD is perfect,'* is direct reference to the absolute, complete, and entire trustworthiness of the Holy Scriptures, which constitute the Bible."

---

[2] From the *Spirit Filled Life Bible*, Thomas Nelson Publishers, page 768.

And this perfect, true, and infallible law, or Word of God, has an effect. The Word of God is active. It revives the soul. God's word literally brings souls back to life.

If, as Paul told Timothy, the Scriptures are God-breathed, then one may ask, "Did the breath of life ever leave them?"

The answer is, "It never has. The Bible is still alive and breathing."

Please forgive me as I indulge in a brief fantasy. Can you visualize this scene? Some unsuspecting soul, let's call him Bob, casually walks into a living room and plunks himself down in a big easy chair. Bob glances over at the side table and notices a Bible lying there. At first he shows no interest. But then suddenly he detects movement. Bob's jaw drops open and his eyes become big as saucers. The Bible is moving. Its pages slowly rise and fall in a rhythmic breathing fashion. In fact, Bob detects the audible sound of escaping breath from the open pages. Our hapless friend catapults from his chair. He bolts from the room screaming, "It's alive! It's alive!"

If only the living nature of God's Word—the aliveness of the Bible—would become that obvious to us all!

When the apostle Paul writes of the God-breathed Scriptures, he is really drawing us into the Genesis imagery regarding the origin of human life: "*The* LORD *God formed the man from the dust of the ground and breathed into his nostrils the breath of life, and the man became a living being*" (Genesis 2:7).

This same LORD God used the same method to bring life to his written Word. The God-breathed Scriptures have a life of their own. Hence the writer of the book of Hebrews declares, "*The word of God is living and active. Sharper than any double-edged sword, it penetrates even to dividing soul and spirit, joints and marrow; it judges the thoughts and attitudes of the heart*" (Hebrews 4:12).

David states in this psalm that the law—and please remember that here the Hebraic understanding of the term *law* refers to the whole of God's written Word—brings revival to the soul. Life begets life. The living Word of God generates spiritual life. As surely as Adam became the father of human life, the written Word of God has been the father of spiritual life since it began its God-breathed, God-initiated existence.

God's Word revives the soul. Adam's seed can initiate biological life, but it takes the Word of God to initiate spirit life inside the human soul. Since Adam's fall, we all enter this world physically alive but spiritually dead.

In Ephesians Paul wrote,

> *As for you, you were dead in your transgressions and sins, in which you used to live when you followed the ways of this world and of the ruler of the kingdom of the air, the spirit who is now at work in those who are disobedient* (Ephesians 2:1–2).

It is God's holy written Word that revives that part of us that died when our first parents disobeyed. Spiritual death occurred the moment Adam and Eve disobeyed. Their obedience to Satan's temptation empowered that ruler of the kingdom of the air. His rulership in the world had its genesis with this first sin. The prince of death established his reign.

Here in this psalm, by God-breathed revelation, this witness speaks of the reviving work of God's Word. When God's Word is brought into contact with the human soul, spirit life springs forth. Our souls are reconnected with our Creator. The harmony between God and man which was lost in the Garden, is suddenly restored.

I am a gardener, and every spring I take dry, dead-looking seeds out of a package and drop them into the soil of my garden. And every spring a certain kind of magic takes place. Those dead-looking seeds come to life and a barren patch of ground becomes an oasis of life and abundance.

That is a picture of God's written Word coming to life in the warm soil of the human heart. A spiritually dead clod of earth suddenly comes alive with the vibrant, pulsating fullness of spirit life—life that comes directly from the Father of lights. There's no experience like it. This is rebirth. This is revival. God's Word is the true source of this life that has been reborn. The living Word has been busy begetting new life.

Now let's return to the premise with which we began this chapter. That premise is that the written Word of God reveals the character of God. Thus far, the second witness has testified to the truth of God's Word. We have learned that God's Word is perfect, hence God is perfect. That perfect Word or law does not leave us dead; instead, it brings revival.

Next, the great witness which is God's Word declares, "*The statutes of the LORD are trustworthy, making wise the simple.*" Only a trustworthy God would give us trustworthy statutes. So God is trustworthy.

Furthermore, through his statutes God imparts wisdom to us. James, the brother of our Lord, invites us to ask for God's wisdom: "*If any of you need wisdom, you should ask God, and it will be given to you. God is generous and won't correct you for asking*" (James 1:5 CEV).

Again the second witness speaks. "*The precepts of the LORD are right, giving joy to the heart.*" Only a righteous God would give us right precepts, so we must logically conclude that God is righteous, or right, in all He does. Furthermore, when the right precepts of this righteous God are applied to the human heart in the context of human relationships and experiences, joy is the result.

In fact, the apostle Paul asserts that, "*the kingdom of God is not a matter of eating and drinking, but of righteousness, peace and joy in the Holy Spirit*" (Romans 14:17).

Real joy—soul-filling and overflowing joy—is rooted in being in right standing with others and with God.

Again the witness of God's Word testifies, "*The commands of the LORD are radiant, giving light to the eyes.*"

If the LORD's commands are radiant, then God, the source of these commands, must be full of light. Here is another characteristic of God that we can add to our growing list. God is light. There is nothing dark or shadowy about Him.

Even as Jesus stooped to impart the gift of sight to a man born blind, he declared, "*I am the light of the world*" (John 9:5).

Are you looking for direction or guidance in this sin-clouded world? Come to Christ, the incarnate Word. Observe God's commands and look to God's Word. The psalmist proclaims, "*Your word is a lamp to my feet and a light for my path*" (Psalm 119:105).

Next our second great witness within this psalm asserts, "*The fear of the LORD is pure, enduring forever.*"

Throughout the Bible we are repeatedly admonished to fear the LORD. "*The fear of the LORD is the beginning of wisdom*" (Proverbs 9:10). Yet we live in a world that ignores the LORD and, even among church-attending believers, the fear of the LORD is a teaching that has fallen much out of fashion. Simultaneously, in far too many of these same churches, sin runs rampant, unchecked and unbridled. Because there is no fear of the LORD, our sanctuaries become polluted.

The fear of the LORD produces purity. James reminds us that "*God is our judge, and he can save or destroy us*" (James 4:12 CEV). If we truly know God as our judge, a holy respect and reverent fear will inform all our thoughts, words, and actions. The fear of the LORD acts as a filter, screening out the impurities the world drops into our lives.

From this statement we can conclude that the eternal God is holy and pure. Because He has designed us to have fellowship with Him, He desires these same qualities in us.

Finally, concerning God's Word, our witness states, "*The ordinances of the LORD are sure and altogether righteous.*"

If God's ordinances are sure and certain, then God must be dependable. We can rely on Him. God's laws are unchanging. God is not evolving; hence His laws are not evolving. Perfection cannot be improved upon.

The writer of Hebrews tells us, "*Jesus Christ is the same yesterday and today and forever*" (Hebrews 13:8). Jesus Christ is as merciful today as He was two thousand years ago. He remains approachable. He is still a healer, a miracle worker, a friend of sinners.

There are no mood swings with God. He is not fickle. He does not change with the times. The changing god, the evolving god who suddenly gets with it, is no god at all, since he is a god fashioned at our own impulse, made to suit and bless our ever-changing whims.

The true God is a Rock—the Rock of truth upon which we can build our lives.

The second witness has spoken. His testimony is a litany of praise for God's Word. Within that litany of praise we discover the character of God. Here is a God who is perfect, trustworthy, righteous, full of light, pure, eternal, and unchanging. But what should excite us most is that this totally wondrous God wants to commune with us, longs to revive us, desires His very best for us. His laws and, by extension, all his written Word are precious beyond compare. Here is the food of heaven for the hungry soul. Jesus said, "*It is written: 'Man does not live on bread alone, but on every word that comes from the mouth of God*' " (Matthew 4:4).

Bringing Life to the Psalms

1. Do you allow time for the witness of God's Word to personally speak into your life? Establish a daily Bible-reading routine. You feed your body daily. Feed your spirit too with a daily dose of Bible reading.

2. Too busy to read God's Word? Buy a set of Bible tapes or CDs and listen to the Word during your daily commute.

3. Post key Bible passages about your home or on your personal computer. Discover ways to embed God's Word into your mind. His Word is life changing as we feed upon it.

4. Can you recall a time when God's Word leapt off the page as you read it? What was that like? What did He say?

The Third Witness Prompts Response

Who can discern his errors?
Forgive my hidden faults.
Keep your servant also from willful sins;
may they not rule over me.
Then will I be blameless,
innocent of great transgression.
May the words of my mouth
and the meditation of my heart
be pleasing in your sight,
O LORD, my Rock and my Redeemer.

WHAT IS YOUR RESPONSE TO God's Word and His voice as it speaks to your heart?

That's exactly what we find here in this final portion of Psalm 19. Here we see David's response to God. So far, God has been doing the talking. He has been speaking to David through the stars, through the night sky and the blazing heat of the sun—the first witness. He has spoken to him through the Word of God, His written revelation—the second witness. Now as this psalm draws to a close we hear David responding to God.

In actuality, David is responding to the third witness. His heart is bearing witness to the reality of God. His conscience is convicting him of his sin and of the righteousness of God. We all have this third witness within us—a witness that will not be silenced, though we may try to drown out this inner voice of the Spirit.

This dialogue between God and man is one of the unique features of the Psalms. They are not simply the statements of a man in prayer, or even the words of a man caught up in praise and worship of his Creator. God speaks back, and as we see in this psalm, God initiates the conversation. We are eavesdropping on a conversation between a human being—someone just like us, caught up in the same travails and passions—and the transcendent, eternal God of the universe.

What a conversation! What communion we find here! This isn't God pronouncing His dictates from heaven, though He has every right to do so. This is God whispering in the ear of an individual who is struggling to know and understand God's will. And if God can speak to David in this manner, then there is hope for us. God can speak to us too. Surely this is why the Psalms have resonated with humankind throughout the ages.

If, along with David, we have heard the voices of the first and second witnesses, then there is only one appropriate response. It is the response recorded here in Holy Scriptures. If we see and grasp the awesome power and majesty of God, and if through His word we have glimpsed His holiness, then we are brought low. We are humbled before Him. Our greatest achievements are nothing. Our pride dissolves. Our weakness, our smallness, is self-evident in the presence of the LORD of heaven and earth. We are exposed; our sin is exposed before this holy, magnificent God.

Hear David's response: "*Who can discern his errors? Forgive my hidden faults.*"

We all stand naked of soul before our Creator. The all-seeing One knows us. He knows us intimately. There are no secrets in His all-encompassing dominion. We can hide nothing from Him.

But hiding is the human heart's first response. Adam and Eve did it first. They hid from their Creator immediately after their initial sin. In fact, hiding is what our Adamic nature does best. Since our first parents' fall, we have had thousands of years to perfect the art of hiding. And it truly is an art. We have all seen and heard a young child's amateurish attempts at a lie, which is simply a verbal attempt at hiding the truth. As we mature we become ever more sophisticated at hiding the truth. We excuse our faults and quickly sweep them under the carpet, and for many of us the thickest and most luxurious carpets are religious carpets. They are great for hiding a multitude of sins.

One of my earliest childhood memories is an attempt to hide from my mother. I hid behind the living room drapes. They were made of thick, heavy material. I could not see her through them, so I reasoned that I must be safe. My feet were left exposed and the form of my body was obvious as I pressed my back against the wall. It's not hard to guess the outcome of this bit of childish foolery.

All of us have tried to play peek-a-boo with God. Our faulty reasoning goes something like this: If I hide from Him and I can't see Him—if I completely ignore Him—He must not be there. I cannot see Him; He cannot see me. He will pass by without noticing me.

But a barefaced encounter with the Almighty exposes all. We have come to the Light. Nothing is hidden, nor can be hidden. We can't play peek-a-boo with God.

David was found by God. He was found naked, just as our first parents were found naked in the Garden. Ah, but that's not what the

Adam and Eve story says. The Bible says, "*they sewed fig leaves together and made coverings for themselves*" (Genesis 3:7).

They were not naked. No, Eve and Adam had managed to pull a curtain over themselves as they hid in God's living room. But their feet were exposed, even as their butts were pressed against the proverbial wall. The truth is, they were naked of soul before the all-seeing God. We are always naked of soul before Him, no matter what outer garb we put on.

Hence, David's first response to God is so appropriate: "*Who can discern his errors? Forgive my hidden faults.*"

With these words, David is giving voice to his inner voice, his conscience. The third witness is testifying to the reality of God—a God before whom we must all give account. The God who speaks externally through creation and His holy written Word also speaks from within the human heart. His voice is prompting David to respond.

David is confessing that before the all-seeing One, he is naked. Not only is he fully exposed, but he is incapable of fully discerning his own sin. He cannot see himself in his entirety. Only God can see him completely.

We should note that our inability to fully see ourselves is true on every level. All too often we are blind to the consequences of our actions, blind to our character faults, blind to the annoying quirks that drive others from us. We cannot stand outside of ourselves and see ourselves fully or accurately. This is as true on the physical level as it is on the spiritual level.

Think on the following statement for a moment: You have never seen your own face. It's true. A photograph of your face is an image of your face caught in time, but it is only an image. It is not your face. The image of your face in a mirror is just that. It is an image; it is not your face. The truth is you have never seen your own face. Only others can see your full physical form.

Only God can see you in your entirety: spirit, soul, and body. He sees you from the outside and from the inside, from your beginning to your end.

In this psalm David finds himself face to face with this all-seeing, all-knowing God. In humility he pleads, *"Forgive my hidden faults."*

If we perceive God correctly, and if we assess ourselves accurately and honestly, then we quickly realize our greatest need—our need for forgiveness. This is the bedrock on which any human relationship with God is built.

Next, because David longs to live in relationship with this amazing God, he cries out for holiness, *"Keep your servant also from willful sins; may they not rule over me. Then will I be blameless, innocent of great transgression"* (Psalm 19:13).

We should note here that there are degrees of sin. For example, John the disciple writes in his first letter, *"There is a sin that leads to death"* (1 John 5:16). John then goes on to state that, *"All wrongdoing is sin, and there is a sin that does not lead to death"* (1 John 5:17).

But perhaps nowhere in all of the Scriptures are the degrees of sin more clearly delineated than here in this passage. David begins by asking, *"Who can discern his errors?"*

There is no intent in errors. We all make mistakes. In this great exam called life, errors will occur. Even the most spiritually studious fall short of perfection. To sin is to miss the mark and all, even the most saintly, will from time to time miss God's mark of perfection.

David asks God to forgive *"hidden sins."* We all possess an ample supply of these. Some sins are hidden from others. We may confess these sins to God, but to others they remain a secret that we take with us to our graves.

Yet other sins are hidden from us. We fail to see our own faults which may be glaringly obvious to others. A truly good friend will not only forgive our faults but, in time, will help us to see and overcome our hidden sins.

As David prays, he asks, "*Keep your servant also from willful sins; may they not rule over me.*"

Here we have transitioned from errors, which are unintentional sins, to the realm of willful sins. This is a conscious decision to do wrong, to disobey God and His laws or requirements. This is a very slippery slope. Notice how willful sin can turn into a controlling monster. We begin by willfully choosing to disobey, but when this sin has taken root and is allowed to grow, something changes. It grows into a monstrosity. What we freely chose now chooses us. We become its slave. It rules over us. Our will is overpowered. Any addict can testify to the ravenous power of this sin monster. Every willful sin has an addictive power associated with it. That's why David wants to avoid this trap. He prays, "*Keep your servant also from willful sins.*"

David longs to be "*blameless, innocent of great transgression.*"

What is great transgression? It could be argued that it is sin that leads to death. James, the brother of our Lord, writes, "*We are tempted by our own desires that drag us off and trap us ... and when sin is finished with us, it leaves us dead*" (James 1:14–15 CEV).

But within David beats a different heart. He longs for holiness. His desire is for a blameless life—a life lived in relationship with God. It's as though David is saying to God, "Those evening walks you took with Adam in the Garden, can we go for one of those, LORD?"

Hear his prayer, "*May the words of my mouth and the meditation of my heart be pleasing in your sight, O LORD, my Rock and my Redeemer.*"

With these words, David identifies the source of sin and the cornerstone of any hope for holiness as we live out our lives on this earth. The source point is the human heart. If our hearts are right before God, there is hope. If our hearts are fixed on our Rock and our Redeemer, we can bring pleasure to Him.

Jesus said, "*The things that come out of the mouth come from the heart, and these make a man 'unclean.' For out of the heart come evil thoughts, murder, adultery, sexual immorality, theft, false testimony, slander. These are what make a man 'unclean'*" (Matthew 15:18–20).

Jesus knew the desperately wicked state of our hearts. David knew his own heart too. He knew it needed cleansing and forgiveness. That's why he cries out for it. He knew that our mouths speak from the overflow of the heart. The meditation of the heart must be pure if the words we speak are to bring life and encouragement.

Your words are important. There is no such thing as an idle word. In a world that constantly spews verbal sewer filth, God is looking for those with a pure heart. Your heavenly Father does not need a stethoscope to check the condition of your heart; he needs only to listen to the words coming out of your mouth.

Notice how David wants his words and his heart to bring pleasure to God. His prayer is that they be pleasing in His sight. Oh, to bring pleasure to the all-seeing One! That is his prayer. He does not wish to hide, as hiding is futile. No, he longs to consciously live his life in the full and constant view of the LORD.

We have all endured annoying music, droning noises, or irritating voices that grate on our nerves. The opposite is so refreshing. Soothing music, joyful noises, and happy voices invigorate us. They bring gladness into our lives.

Like David, make it your goal to bring gladness to your Rock and your Redeemer. Put a smile on your Father's face.

Bringing Life to the Psalms

1. Read James 2:1–12. There is no clearer biblical discourse on the power of the tongue for both good and evil. Heed the advice found there.
2. Do you have a foul mouth? Determine to clean up your conversation. When you slip up, make Psalm 19:14 your prayer.

3. Is the third witness—the inner voice of God's Spirit—speaking to you? Take time to respond to God. Use David's prayer in this final portion of Psalm 19 as a pattern for your own response to the Holy Spirit's prompting.

4. Take time to meditate on God's Word. Select a passage and read it repeatedly. See it. Smell it. Taste it. Let it become part of you. In our rushed world, become a cow: lie down, relax, and chew your mental cud. Meditating on God's Word is like that.

5. Now take a minute to reread all of Psalm 19. What is God saying to you by His Spirit?

The Good Life

A psalm of David

The LORD is my shepherd,
I shall not be in want.
He makes me lie down in green pastures,
he leads me beside quiet waters,
he restores my soul.
He guides me in paths of righteousness
for his name's sake.

YESTERDAY I WENT FOR A LONG and pleasant walk through Lincoln Park, which straddles Lake Michigan in Chicago. It was a perfect summer day. Children were playing on the long sandy beach. Waves danced in the sunlight.

From that weekday afternoon stroll, a number of vignettes remain cemented in my mind. There were the four strapping young men caught up in a game of beach volleyball. Another fine-looking young man rolled by me on his bicycle. Later I saw him stretched out on the seawall, stripped to his shorts, perfecting his tan. Down by the marina, two attractive young ladies in bathing suits were in animated conversation as I walked by. One of them even glanced my way. Farther on, sitting on a park bench, a first-time father dandled and bounced his blond two-year-old on his knees. The beaming lad greeted me with a smile that simply invited conversation. Still at the marina, a middle-aged couple parked their Cadillac SUV. Later I saw them sail their yacht out of the bay. It was a perfect day for sailing.

Ah, the good life! There is nothing like it. People in pursuit of the good life: that's what I was watching. In fact, that's what I myself was enjoying—a slice of the good life.

The truth is, all of us want the good life. Is that a wrong desire? Or is it simply the way God made us? We want a life filled with pleasant experiences—a life we can look back on and say, "Now that was a life worth living. That was a good life!"

Somehow, many of us have developed a rather perverse view of God. Isn't He that supreme killjoy in the sky? Doesn't He get His kicks by shutting down anything resembling fun? We have this sense that if we are enjoying ourselves too much, God somehow can't be in it. Has God become for you a severe, demanding taskmaster?

Is that a correct, biblical view of God? And what does all this have to do with Psalm 23? Well, if there is a biblical recipe or prescription for the good life, I would say that it can be found in the words of this psalm. It is a psalm that drips with satisfaction. It oozes with the very fullness of life; it overflows with a quiet peace. There is a mellow ripeness to these words that runs down your chin, lights a spark in your eye, and puts a spring in your step.

"The LORD is my shepherd, I shall not be in want."

The first line is the key to it all. Is the LORD your Shepherd? If He is, then all the rest follows. The fullness, the goodness, the love simply come trailing along behind Him as you follow in His steps. This is so easy, so obvious. But you can miss it, because it seems far too simple.

We live in a world that is in feverish pursuit of the good life. The self-centered pursuit of happiness has become the crowning but ever-illusive goal. The word *pursuit* says it all. Apparently, happiness is something we are to chase after. According to this life model, more is always better and to settle for sufficiency is to settle for second best. The race is on. To the winner goes the ever-retreating prize. Oops! There it goes. It just slipped over the next hill.

What a profoundly different model for the good life is found within the words of this psalm. The good life, which in our hearts we all seek, is anchored in the Good Shepherd. Jesus is that Good Shepherd. Listen to His words, *"I am the good shepherd; I know my sheep, and my sheep know me"* (John 10:14).

It is in following Him rather than following our own desires, that happiness comes. There is an abundance that comes into play the moment we surrender our stubborn will to the Good Shepherd. Now hear the promise in David's words: *"I shall not be in want."*

There is freedom from worry contained in those words. He is the Shepherd of "more-than-enough." One Bible translation puts this promise of sufficiency this way; *"I don't need a thing"* (THE MESSAGE). David sees himself as amply supplied. That is the very nature of the Good Shepherd. He will always make sure His followers have more than enough.

It is worth noting that Jesus' first great sermon zeroed right in on this concept of freedom from worry. He wanted His disciples, His followers, to fully understand this, so He taught that He who clothes the grass of the field will clothe them as well. He who feeds the birds will be sure to provide food for them as well. This freedom from worry is not rooted in some mindless feel-good sloganeering. No, it is rooted in the sure and dependable promise of God. Hear Jesus as he throws out the challenge to all of us: *"Seek first his kingdom and his righteousness, and all these other things will be given to you as well"* (Matthew 6:33).

The Good Shepherd is still calling His sheep. Those who hear His voice and follow will know the full meaning of the words, *"I shall not be in want."*

To a world caught up in chasing after happiness, the Good Shepherd brings rest.

"He makes me lie down in green pastures; he leads me beside quiet waters."

Our God is a God of rest. Rest was His idea. The Almighty was not exhausted by the work of creation. He did not rest on the seventh day because He was plumb tuckered out. He rested for our sakes, to teach us a permanent lesson on the value of rest and relaxation. He beckons us to come away to the quiet waters.

There is something calming about a body of water. There is a therapy to be found at the water's edge. Water at rest brings rest to the weary soul. There is a kind of divine magic that quiet water can work upon our frazzled psyche. I dare say all of us have felt its power.

"He restores my soul."

Oh, what promise there is in these words! Can you hear the Good Shepherd calling? Listen to His beckoning call, *"Come to me, all you who are weary and burdened, and I will give you rest"* (Matthew 11:28).

To the world weary, to the chasers after fleeting pleasure, to those battered by disappointment, to those trapped in the downward spiral of sin, Jesus is calling. To those who hear and follow He brings rest. And with that rest comes restoration.

There is a great redeeming lesson here. We are not saved by our good works. A never-ending cycle of human effort will not open heaven's door. Instead, the door is opened when we come to rest—rest in Jesus—rest in the nail-scarred hands of the Good Shepherd. He has done the work for us. Now we just come and rest in Him. Our souls' salvation is a rest. It's not a work. It is not achieved by our efforts because salvation's source is not in us, but in Him.

The Good Shepherd is in the complete restoration business. He restores souls burned out by addiction, brings hope to the depressed, gives victory to the defeated and imperishable value to those tossed out on the trash heap of society.

"He restores my soul." Has He restored your soul? If you put your soul in His hands, Jesus will do the work.

"He guides me in paths of righteousness for his name's sake."

Here we see the shepherd in his most visible and obvious role. He is the guide, the leader of the flock. He takes the sheep out to pasture and then back to the sheepfold. Have you surrendered the leadership role in your life to the Good Shepherd? Are your decisions made in full submission to the LORD? Are you the leader or is He?

This is not a decision that is settled once for all time. On the contrary; this is a daily, conscious decision to follow where the Good Shepherd leads. Where He leads today may be totally different from where He leads tomorrow. Are you willing to change course? Are your ears open to hear the Shepherd's call?

David grew up doing the work of a shepherd, so we can assume he knew a great deal about sheep. One of the distinguishing features of sheep is their predisposition to flock together and be followers. Goats, on the other hand, are a stubborn, ornery, and independent lot. They follow no one. They are masters of their own destiny. Are you a goat or a sheep?

Men in particular are raised to be independent, self-directed leaders. Surrendering leadership to someone else runs contrary to our upbringing, what we have been taught in school, how we have been socialized, and our natural disposition. But that is exactly what the Lord asks us to do.

It is precisely this aspect of Psalm 23 which personally gives me the most trouble. You see, I always think I know what is best for me. Why should I let someone else decide what is best for my life? Yes, in my mind I can tell myself that God is good and that He will be good to me, but He is not living in my skin, facing my problems, or confined to the limitations that I encounter.

But wait just a minute. Let's examine those three objections one by one.

"He is not living in my skin." That is an outright lie spawned by the devil. I invited Christ into my heart. He is in residence there. Jesus is in fact living in my skin. He is at work within me, helping me daily to live out His characteristics and attributes. The apostle Paul writes, *"Christ lives in me. The life I live in the body, I live by faith in the Son of God, who loved me and gave himself for me"* (Galatians 2:20). In effect, what Paul is saying is that the Good Shepherd laid down His life for me, has taken up residence within me and, as I live by faith, will pilot me on the right course for my life.

Now let's look at the second objection. *"He's not facing my problems."* This can only be true if I have if I have blocked my ears to the Good Shepherd's call and if I am hastily trotting off in the opposite direction. Please keep in mind that choosing to cut and run is an option which any believer can choose at any time. You see, when I first surrendered to Christ, a huge vacuum cleaner did not descend from the sky and suck the brains out of my head. My brain was not replaced by a circuit board connected wirelessly to the Great Central Control up in the sky. My decision to follow Jesus must be renewed daily. The Good Shepherd leaves my free will intact. I am always free to choose or reject Him and His plan for my life.

If I truly belong to the Good Shepherd, then my problems are His problems. He is my burden bearer. I am yoked with Him. Jesus and I form a two-man team. Listen to His words, *"Take my yoke upon you and learn from me, for I am gentle and humble in heart, and you will find rest for your souls. For my yoke is easy and my burden is light"* (Matthew 11:29–30).

The Good Shepherd is gentle and humble, not harsh and demanding. As I bring my problems to Him, I find they are lighter. He carries the heavy end while I find the rest that I desperately need.

Now what about that last objection, *"He is not confined to the limitations that I encounter."* This objection presumes that Jesus is unsympathetic about the obstacles and difficulties I face in life. Over and over again I am frustrated by my limited resources, lack of time, and an inability to see what the future holds. The truth is, that is precisely why I need to submit my life to the Good Shepherd. He knows the future, can supply limitless resources, and can arrange my time for maximum benefit. When I choose to follow Him, He knows exactly what is over the next hill. Furthermore, He has made provision in advance. Why then, do I foolishly cling to the mistaken notion that I know what is best, when I am blind to what lies ahead? Pride and a lack of trust are the most likely causes of this spiritual shortsightedness.

To experience the good life into which the Good Shepherd would lead us, we must humble ourselves and follow. We must trust that He is truly good all the time, even in times when we do not understand His leading or why He has us walking on a particular path. I have found that, in time, as I submit and follow, He makes all things clear. He can be trusted.

Finally we need to recognize the full truth of the words, *"He guides me in paths of righteousness for his name's sake."* The paths He chooses for us are paths of righteousness. Righteousness is not always the easiest path. We can be sure it is the best path, but the easiest? We have no guarantee of that. Doing the right thing does not always lead to accolades from our peers or those above us in rank or responsibility. But ultimately, our accountability is to a much higher authority. The Good Shepherd reminds us that, *"wide is the gate and broad the road that leads to destruction, and many enter through it. But small is the gate and narrow the road that leads to life, and only a few find it"* (Matthew 7:13–14). Jesus is the guide along that narrow road.

Remember that Jesus has you walking paths of righteousness *for his name's sake.* The good life is about bringing glory and honor to Him. You see, it's not about you or me at all. It's all about Him. The good life cannot be lived for self. It must be lived for Jesus and others. That's where the blessing is. The richest lives are the poured out lives. They overflow with goodness, love, and peace because they have tapped into the ocean of God.

Bringing Life to the Psalms

1. Consider reading a biography of a person who truly lived the good life. People like Hudson Taylor, Mother Teresa, William Wilberforce, Helen Keller, and Martin Luther King spring to my mind. Perhaps you can think of others who heard the Good Shepherd and then followed with all their heart.

2. Plan a rest break, preferably beside some quiet water. Use some of that rest time to read, reread, and meditate on Psalm 23.

3. Have you left the path Jesus has for you? If He is calling you back, make this the day you heed His voice and follow Him anew.

You Are With Me

*Even though I walk through the valley of the
shadow of death,
I will fear no evil,
for you are with me;
your rod and your staff,
they comfort me.
You prepare a table before me
in the presence of my enemies.
You anoint my head with oil;
my cup overflows.
Surely goodness and love will follow me
all the days of my life,
and I will dwell in the house of the
LORD forever.*

I AM ALONE TONIGHT, AND I AM
800 miles (1,300 kilometers) from home. One of my adult sons
came with me on this trip to Chicago, but he left this afternoon for
an overnight side trip with a friend. It rained all day, leaving me

trapped indoors. I was hoping for some change in the weather so I could go for a walk this evening, but the drizzle continues. I responded to an e-mail from my wife, but now I'm alone with my thoughts.

Life does not always hand us sunny days. I am reminded of that as I turn to this portion of Psalm 23. As we follow the Good Shepherd, He may take us on a path we would not willingly choose. The valley of the shadow of death alludes to events and situations more serious than a bit of rainy-day blues. The loss of a parent, a child, or a life partner is a deep valley indeed. But David's response is most interesting. He confidently states, *"I will fear no evil, for you are with me."*

But I can hear the incredulous skeptics asking, "David, you're not afraid of evil? Don't you know there is an enormous amount of evil out on the loose in this world? There is cancer. There's AIDS and dementia. There are terrorists on the loose. Crime is rampant. Families are disintegrating. Our nation's youth are going to hell in a filth-laced, hip hop-spouting hand basket. David, you need to tune in to the news. There are wars and rumors of wars, earthquakes and famines. We are living in the end times."

To all this David's reply is the same, *"I will fear no evil, for you are with me."*

David's confidence is unshaken. It is unshaken because he knows the Good Shepherd. He knows Him well. And we can know Him too. Jesus is not a fair-weather friend who disappears at the first hint of trouble. No, when the times get tough, He draws all the closer. During our darkest hour He holds us closest.

We need to remember who penned this psalm. David repeatedly went through times of horrific loss. After achieving victory after victory, he lost favor with King Saul and had to flee for his life. He lost the affection of his first wife. He endured years of deprivation as he was hunted like a common criminal. At one point, he lost favor with his own men and they were about to stone him. Jonathan, his dearest friend, was killed in battle. David's own beloved son led a revolt against him and sought to kill him. His closest friends and advisers turned away from him. He mourned the death of two of his sons. David was all too well acquainted with the valley of death. He descended its steep slopes on many occasions.

But despite all this he assures us, *"I will fear no evil, for you are with me."*

You see, David was never alone. In his darkest hour, the Bible records, *"David found strength in the LORD his God"* (1 Samuel 30:6). During those terrible times, the Good Shepherd was near. David was in the service of the God who is with us.

David asserts, *"Your rod and your staff, they comfort me."*

During those difficult times, David drew comfort from the LORD's presence right there beside him. There are really two aspects to be considered when we look at the statement, *"Your rod and your staff, they comfort me."* Both aspects are protective. On the one hand the Good Shepherd provides protection against the encroaching intruder; on the other hand He protects us from ourselves.

Let's look at the encroaching intruder first. I have spent enough time trekking about the forested wilderness of Canada to draw a certain comfort from carrying a good, sturdy stick. There is no telling what you may encounter around the next bend or over the next ridge. Not all wildlife fits under the category of small and cute.

As a shepherd, David was keenly aware of predators that might harm his flock. Listen to David's boldness as he tells Saul how he defended his own flock of sheep:

> *Your servant has been keeping his father's sheep.*
> *When a lion or a bear came and carried off a*
> *sheep from the flock, I went after it, struck it and*
> *rescued the sheep from its mouth. When it turned*

on me, I seized it by its hair, struck it and killed it.
Your servant has killed both the lion and the
bear ... (1 Samuel 17:34–36).

David knew how to use the rod to defend and rescue his flock. He himself was rescued from certain death time and time again by the Good Shepherd. The proverbial cat with nine lives had nothing on David. As you read first and second Samuel, you come to realize how frequently David escaped from the jaws of death. He knew the comfort of the Shepherd's rod.

Oh, what a tenacious Shepherd we serve! The Good Shepherd fights for His sheep. The roaring lion may approach, but Jesus says, *"No one can snatch them out of my hand"* (John 10:28). There is a wonderful security in which we can rest as we follow this heaven-sent Shepherd.

Let's examine the second protective aspect we see in this statement, *"Your rod and your staff, they comfort me."*

The LORD, who is my Shepherd, protects me from myself. Sheep are not the brightest stars in the firmament. Intellectually, they do not rank very high in the animal kingdom. Some would go so far as to say that they are rather stupid. Consequently, sheep are apt to put themselves in harm's way rather than having the prudence to avoid it.

Though collectively, humanity sits on top of the intellectual heap, our innate ability to make stupid decisions is renowned. The annual Darwin Awards are a testimony to the ridiculously stupid things people do—actions stupid enough to get the instigators killed. This definitely is one award list on which you do not want your name to appear.

I confess that I have made enough dumb mistakes to fill every page of this book. Please excuse me for not providing all the details. If you have lived long enough and have kept good records, you could probably do the same. Our daily prayer needs to be, "Dear Lord Jesus, please save me from myself."

(Curiously, within two hours of writing the above paragraph, I locked my keys in my car. Lord, did I really need a fresh reminder of my ability to make dumb mistakes? I rest my case.)

In the spiritual realm, we are particularly blind to danger. We prance right over to the newest trap the devil has set for us. Snares? Pitfalls? What are those? We butt, shove, and jostle the other sheep so we can get the best possible cliff-side view. Spiritual danger? What's that?

The Good Shepherd wields the shepherd's staff for good reason. He needs that staff to pull us back to safety. I am sure that the pastor of every church in the land could come up with a list of candidates for a Christian version of the Darwin Awards. To my shame, I might make that list myself.

"Dear Lord Jesus, please save me from myself."

Where would I be if the Good Shepherd lost His staff? May my grateful confession always be, *"Your rod and your staff, they comfort me."*

David continues, *"You prepare a table before me in the presence of my enemies."*

The stark truth is Satan and his cohorts have me surrounded. There is trouble and disaster lurking on every side. But in the middle of all this, Jesus has prepared a feast for me—a banquet table spread with the most nutritious and delectable fare. There is the fresh-daily bread of heaven—the Word of God. For the parched soul there is an endless supply of the water of life. Every fruit of the Spirit is there in abundance. And this Good Shepherd, who laid down His life for the sheep, has put His own body and blood on that banquet table. Now with a nail-scarred hand outstretched, He beckons, "Come. Come, my beloved. Come and dine."

Oh, don't neglect His invitation. He will meet you there. As you dine, be ever mindful of His words, *"Whoever eats my flesh and drinks my blood has eternal life, and I will raise him up at the last day"* (John 6:54).

David declares, *"You anoint my head with oil."*

Surely as David penned these particular words, his mind recalled the most significant event of his life. No, it wasn't the day he slew Goliath, or the day he was crowned king of all Israel and Judah. It was the day that the venerable old prophet, Samuel, dropped in on Jesse and his family for a visit. David, being the youngest son, was nearly overlooked as he was out tending the sheep. Let's take a brief look at what happened that day.

"Samuel took the horn of oil and anointed him in the presence of his brothers, and from that day on the Spirit of the LORD came upon David in power" (1 Samuel 16:13).

This particular passage makes it clear that all the great accomplishments of David's life flowed from this singular experience. The Spirit of the LORD came upon David, and he killed the lion and the bear. The Spirit of the LORD came upon David, and he slew Goliath. The Spirit of the LORD came upon David, and he defeated the Philistines time and time again. And on and on it goes. There was a power source that came into David's life that day, a power which defies natural explanation. It came as he was anointed, and the passage makes it abundantly clear that this power source was the Spirit of the LORD.

David was anointed for a purpose. That purpose was to serve and lead the people of Israel. In due time that anointing brought him to the throne room. Has God anointed you to serve? Has the Holy Spirit come upon you in power?

Just a few hours ago I returned from a cycling excursion. It is about seven miles (eleven kilometers) from where I am staying here in Chicago to the downtown. I set out at a leisurely pace along beautiful Lakeshore Park. My pace quickened as I neared Navy Pier, my turnaround point at the downtown core. This part of the trip was a breeze. After a brief rest I headed back. That's when I discovered why the trip downtown had been so easy. The wind had been at my back. They don't call Chicago the windy city without cause. My whole body was a sail pushing me in the opposite direction. I put in twice the effort and achieved half the results.

Trying to do God's work and will without the help of the Holy Spirit is just like that. But when the wind of God's Spirit is at your back, there is real power in every stride you take. David experienced the anointing of the Good Shepherd and it totally transformed his life. The same Good Shepherd has an anointing for you as well.

When God's anointing is present in someone's life, their cup overflows. David's experience can be yours as well. The good life that comes from following the Good Shepherd is an overflowing life. The Good Shepherd supplies more than enough joy, more than enough peace, more than enough love, mercy, and forgiveness.

Take God at His word. As you follow the Good Shepherd, expect goodness and love to follow you all the days of your life. Following Jesus is not intended to be a temporary measure, and neither is His blessing on your life intended to be temporary. His desire for you is a good life—a good life that extends through all eternity.

Hear David's finally confident declaration: *"I will dwell in the house of the LORD forever."*

The Good Shepherd prepared a place for David. It's a place in the household of God. Before His departure Jesus told all of His followers that *"in my Father's house are many rooms; if it were not so, I would have told you. I am going there to prepare a place for you"* (John 14:2).

David is occupying a room in that big house right now, and some great day in the future I plan to walk by that room. I expect I will hear a trickling noise, or maybe it will even be a gushing noise coming from behind that door. That's because I am sure of this one thing: David's wonderful cup is still overflowing.

Bringing Life to the Psalms

1. Consider reading the biblical account of David's life found in the Old Testament books of First and Second Samuel. These books provide a wonderful backdrop for any study of the Psalms.

2. David was anointed for a purpose. Have you discovered how God wants you to serve Him? Take time to pray for clarity in this regard. Too many of God's people are wandering aimlessly, while He longs to anoint them powerfully for specific service.

3. Pull up a chair to the Lord's banquet table. Be sure to read a portion of God's Word every day. Make the celebration of the Lord's Supper a regular part of your corporate worship routine.

4. Take a minute to reread this entire incomparable psalm. What is the Good Shepherd saying to you by His Spirit?

Breaking the Dam

A psalm of David

Blessed is he whose transgressions are forgiven,
whose sins are covered.
Blessed is the man whose sin the LORD does not
count against him
and in whose spirit is no deceit.
When I kept silent,
my bones wasted away through my groaning
all day long.
For day and night your hand was heavy
upon me;
my strength was sapped as in the heat of
summer. (Selah)
Then I acknowledged my sin to you
and did not cover up my iniquity.
I said, "I will confess my transgressions to
the LORD"—
and you forgave the guilt of my sin. (Selah)

BEAVERS ARE CERTAINLY AMONG the most intelligent and industrious of all of God's creatures. They are ingenious designers and builders of both homes and dams which completely transform the environment in which they live. Only humans outperform them in this regard. In the wilderness, their activity and its effects are a sight well worth seeing.

To the rural property owner, however, the arrival of beavers can turn into a disaster of appalling proportions. The gently flowing stream that was a source of much pleasure is now blocked. Prized trees are being felled by these industrious little devils on a daily basis. Acres of valuable land are being turned into fetid swamp. As the dam's reservoir rises, hundreds more trees succumb to drowning; their stark branches and dead trunks punctuate the sky. A blocked stream can produce an atrocious mess.

A right relationship with God is like a flowing stream. In such a relationship, there is a natural giving to God that includes prayer, worship, time spent in His Word, and periods of quiet communion. In turn God, by the Holy Spirit, pours His peace, love, and joy into our lives. And just as trees naturally line a river bank, there is a verdant fruitfulness that comes to the believer as that refreshing current is allowed to flow.

Sin acts like a boulder, hindering the flow of God's Spirit in our lives. As more and more unrepented sin piles up, a dam is formed. Suddenly prayer stops. Worship and thanksgiving that once cascaded so freely from our lips comes to a halt. The Word of God becomes boring, and we find other interests. Times of quiet communion with our Maker are replaced by a search for other things or for constant entertainment.

Let's read David's description of the spiritual swamp his life became because of unconfessed sin.

"When I kept silent, my bones wasted away through my groaning all day long. For day and night your hand was heavy upon me. My strength was sapped as in the heat of summer."

The flow had stopped. Where was the overflowing cup experience of Psalm 23? At this point David's cup—his soul—was sitting stagnant. And in the natural realm any liquid left unstirred becomes foul as time goes by.

As I write this, I can see a small coffee table on the veranda below me, and on that table sits a bottle of orange juice. I first noticed this bottle exactly a week ago when I arrived here in Chicago. After passing this bottle several times on the way up to my room, I became curious and went over for a closer inspection. That's when I discovered why the bottle was there. It was acting as a paperweight to keep a hand-written note from blowing away. No one would move the bottle in the hope that the unknown person to whom the note was addressed would finally show up. In the past few days, due to the summer sun and heat, the orange juice has taken on a rather brown hue.

Judging from David's comment regarding the strength-sapping heat of summer, we might assume that the contents of his soul had taken on a rather brown hue as well. The problem was, he kept silent. Sin has a way of silencing our relationship with God. We are not told what sin or transgression produced this damming effect. Yet that is just what it was. A dam caused by sin was now completely blocking David's relationship with God.

Perhaps it is better that we don't know the particulars of David's transgression, as a sense of personal spiritual superiority might set in. But sin is sin. Sin in any of its various forms fouls our relationship with God. James reminds us that a single sin can have huge conse-quences: *"For whoever keeps the whole law and yet stumbles at just one point is guilty of breaking all of it"* (James 2:10).

What can break the sin dam and bring us back into a right relationship with God? David discovered the answer within this psalm. Hear his pivotal words: *"Then I acknowledged my sin to you and did not cover up my iniquity. I said, 'I will confess my transgres-sions to the* LORD.'"

Confession breaks the dam. David verbally brought his sin out in the open before God. He acknowledged what God knew all along. You see, David's sin was not hidden from God. It was in plain sight of the LORD from the moment of its conception.

Once again the words of James are very instructive in this regard as he states, "*each one is tempted when, by his own evil desire, he is dragged away and enticed. Then, after desire has conceived, it gives birth to sin, and sin, when it is full-grown, gives birth to death*" (James 1:14–15).

Sin was already working with deadly effect on David's soul. By his own admission, his bones were wasting away and his strength was sapped. Only a dam-busting experience could bring David back into right relationship with God and restore the flow of praise, prayer, and worship that had once been there.

One of the critical Allied successes of World War II was the June 16, 1944, RAF raid on the Mohne and Eder dams on the Ruhr River system in Germany. To break the dams, specially- designed spinning cylindrical bombs were created by British inventor Barnes Wallis. Those huge bombs were dropped by specially-modified Lancaster bombers from a height of 60 feet (18 meters). The bombs hit and skipped across the surface of the water of the dam's reservoir. They then slammed into the back of the dam, began to sink, and then exploded with massive dam-busting force. A decisive victory was achieved that night as those dam-busting bombs unleashed their power.

Fortunately, God has equipped each of us with dam-busting bombs to destroy the spiritual dams in our life—dams that our own sins have built. Words of confession and contrite acknowledgement are dam-busters. They break strongholds of sin, and in so doing they release the putrid dead waters that have backed up into our lives.

It is well worth noting that these putrid dead waters can be the cause of actual physical disease within our bodies. The human spirit is inextricably linked to the human body, and when our spiritual man or woman is sick due to unrepented sin, physical ailments and sickness can often follow. They are the natural by-products of a sin-blocked spirit.

When David states, "*my bones were wasting away, and my strength was sapped as in the heat of summer,*" we can see these words simply as a nice poetic touch. The stark reality, however, is that spiritual sickness can produce a plethora of physical symptoms. Doctors have been aware of this link for many years now.

Again the brother of our Lord has much to say on this point. Let's look at his thoughts on this topic:

> *If you are sick, ask the church leaders to come and pray for you. Ask them to put olive oil on you in the name of the Lord. If you have faith when you pray for sick people, they will get well. The Lord will heal them, and if they have sinned, he will forgive them. If you have sinned, you should tell each other what you have done. Then you can pray for one another and be healed* (James 5:14–16 CEV).

What stands out most clearly in this passage is the link between physical healing and forgiveness. Confession is the bridge that re-establishes our link to God, and it is God who is the source of both forgiveness and healing. Re-establish the link, and the current of God's grace can once again flow into your life.

I do dramatizations of the Epistle of James, and it is always amazing to hear accounts of what happens when God's people put His Word into action. In one case, a pastor contacted me to report how a young woman in his congregation was miraculously healed of rheumatoid arthritis after watching me doing a dramatization of James. She acted on the Word of God. Her relationship with her father had completely broken down. After confessing her faults and seeking restoration, God not only healed that relationship, but also healed her of the arthritis that had been crippling her body for years. The sin dam was broken and God flooded her body with healing.

Can you hear the joy in David's voice as he announces to the world, "*And you forgave the guilt of my sin*"?

The forgiveness of God is amazing. It breaks the chains of sin's bondage. There is no liberation like the liberation of full and free forgiveness. It frees the tormented soul from guilt, and sets the liberated individual on the path to heaven, the very path that all the saints have trod. Oh, that our nation would be awakened by the joyous cry of liberated sinners. We need a society-changing sinners' liberation.

David experienced the dam-busting, soul-liberating power of the LORD's forgiveness. It is little wonder, then, that he begins this psalm by announcing, "*Blessed is he whose transgressions are forgiven, whose sins are covered. Blessed is the man whose sin the LORD does not count against him and in whose spirit is no deceit.*"

David knew this blessed state of forgiveness. Now for him, the long ledger of sin has been wiped clean. The debt has been paid. All who find themselves in such a position are truly blessed.

Yesterday's gospel reading at my home church in Ottawa was the Beatitudes from Jesus' sermon on the mount. Each beatitude begins with the phrase, "*Blessed are …*" I wonder if, in His mind, Jesus was using the opening lines of Psalm 32 as His springboard for launching into the Beatitudes. The blessed state of the forgiven is certainly a key theme throughout Jesus' teaching and ministry.

There is a rather curious statement in the opening lines of this psalm, and it is made in regard to our sins being covered. We are wonderfully blessed when our sins are covered. Yet only a few lines down, David laments the fact that he tried to cover up his iniquity. On the one hand he is saying that our sin being covered is a good thing, and on the other hand covering our sins is terrible. David, what do you mean?

The question we need to ask ourselves is, "Who is covering my sin?"

If you are covering your sin, it is an abomination—an affront to God. God can see your sin and any amount of cover-up that you attempt is utter foolishness before the all-seeing, all-knowing LORD of the universe. Before Him the whole of it is always fully exposed. David's attempt to hide his iniquity was an act of sheer stupidity. Any of our attempts at hiding our sin fall under the same category. It is a form of spiritual deceit. We must bring our sins out into the open before God. That is what David eventually did, and that was when forgiveness flowed. At that moment, David entered that blessed state—the blessed state of the forgiven.

But what happens to that exposed sin? God covers it. As believers who stand on this side of the cross, we know that Jesus covers it with His blood. Only the all-seeing, all-knowing God can cover our sin so well that even He cannot find it.

God gave us a lesson in sin covering on its very first occurrence in Genesis. Adam and Eve hid and covered their nakedness with fig leaves. Their cover-up was not acceptable to the LORD back then, even as our cover-up is unacceptable to Him now. We read, *"The LORD God made garments of skin for Adam and his wife and clothed them"* (Genesis 3:21).

The LORD covered them. He shed the blood of an animal to provide a covering of skins for them. Because I need a covering today, two thousand years ago the LORD God shed the blood of His one and only Son so that I too could be covered. Oh, what a blessed covering that is!

Because of Jesus I am blessed. I am forgiven! How about you?

Bringing Life to the Psalms

1. Words of contrite confession are like dam-busting bombs. Are there unconfessed sins clogging and hindering your relationship with God? Make it your first priority to confess those sins to God. If your relationship with others has been affected, seek reconciliation with them. God desires that all our relationships be healthy and filled with the free-flowing life of His Spirit.

2. Do a James 5 health check. If you are sick or disabled in any way, ask the church leaders to anoint you with oil and pray for you. *"Jesus Christ is the same yesterday and today and forever"* (Hebrews 13:8). His healing grace is available to those who humbly call on Him. And remember, He still makes house calls.

3. Read the Beatitudes as recorded in Matthew 5:3–12. Consider possible attitudinal links to Psalm 32.

4. If forgiveness is a key theme in Jesus' ministry and teaching, can you think of accounts in the Gospels that reflect this? Are you stumped? Here are a few quick references to check out: Mark 2:1–12; Luke 23:39–43; Luke 19:1–10; Luke 7:36–50; Luke 18:9–14

The Hidden God and the Hiding Place

Therefore let everyone who is godly pray to you
while you may be found;
surely when the mighty waters rise,
they will not reach him.
You are my hiding place;
you will protect me from trouble
and surround me with songs of deliverance.

IN THE PREVIOUS STANZA OF this psalm, David had just received the marvelous dam-busting forgiveness of God. Can you hear the excitement still ringing in David's voice? He has just experienced a wonderful release from a load of guilt. Then in his next breath he has some advice for us, and here it is: *"Therefore let everyone who is godly pray to you, while you may be found."*

We are to pray to God while He may be found. This raises some interesting questions. Is God unavailable at times? If God cannot be found, is He hiding? Furthermore, if God is hiding, where does He hide?

At this point I feel like jumping to my feet like a lawyer in the court of reason, and shouting out, "I object! All that David has told us about God so far would lead us to believe that God is always close at hand. Didn't David testify to this earlier in Psalm 23? He said the following words about the LORD his Shepherd: *'Even though I walk through the valley of the shadow of death, I will fear no evil, for you are with me.'* And now it seems David is telling us that there are times when God cannot be found. Which is it, David? It can't be both."

Ah, but it is both. This is one of those great divine paradoxes. The God who is near, even in my heart, can also be distant—light years away—both in time and place. There exists a perceived distance between us that can vary accord to the state of my heart; that is, according to the state of my relationship with God.

The fact remains that we cannot see God. We can see evidence of His handiwork all around us. Our infinitely complex human bodies and finely tuned senses are themselves proof of His existence, yet we cannot see Him. He is a hidden God, and when we walk beside Him, we walk by faith and not by sight.

Repeatedly in the Scriptures we are commanded to seek after the LORD. I find this to be a rather curious expression. We cannot see God, and yet we are commanded to seek Him, as though He might suddenly appear over the next hill or around the next bend in the road. Suddenly, in unexpected ways, we may encounter God. In reality, the Psalms are all about encounters with God. Psalm 19 began that way. Suddenly the starry hosts began talking to David about

God, declaring His glory. We may pick up the Bible and suddenly it speaks to our deepest need—the need of the moment—and we know that this is the voice of God with a word specifically for us today.

Even the ungodly people of this world recognize that people encounter God. They use expressions like, "He found God," to describe someone's conversion to faith in Christ.

As a young lad growing up on a farm in Saskatchewan, I had a very frightening experience that left me totally baffled for several days. I was about eleven years old at the time, and my younger brother, who always accompanied me, was about nine. During our summer vacation we loved to tramp about the wooded pastureland that surrounded our farm home. In the far corner of the pasture we found a secluded spot where we chopped down a few saplings and set up a makeshift tent.

My dog, Champ, always tagged along on these excursions. On one of these outings, while we were relaxing by our tent, Champ went totally berserk. He began barking frantically. He ran in tight circles around us. Every hair on his back stood erect. He was totally panicked.

We looked about to see what had set the dog into such a sudden frenzy, but could see nothing. His urgent alarm grew even more intense. The dog was completely beside himself with fear as he continued to run circles around us. Each frantic bark urged us out of there. I picked up the axe and together we ran for our lives. From what we ran, my brother and I could only guess. Was it some large wild animal? A malicious human intruder? I had never seen my dog react this way to anything or anyone.

We reported this event to our parents who listened with interest, but they could offer no further insight except to say that it was wise to heed Champ's warning and leave. We were spooked by this event, and did not return to our favorite spot for well over a week.

Finally, we took courage and, on a sunny summer afternoon, set out for our secluded campsite once again. Of course Champ tagged along with us. All went well until we were very near our destination. As we emerged into an open grassy area, Champ suddenly went ballistic. But this time I clearly saw the cause of his alarm. There, a short distance ahead, a huge tawny cat—a cougar—reared up and bounded off into the woods.

We froze in our tracks. We were shaken to the core. But now we knew what was out there. On that earlier occasion, only my faithful dog stood between us and that powerful predator. Without his fierce protection, two prairie boys may well have become a hungry cougar's lunch and supper.

In a peculiar way, an unexpected encounter with the living God can be a lot like an encounter with a cougar. Suddenly, we realize our every move has been studied and watched; we are not alone. And that other being out there, watching us, is much bigger and more powerful than we are. Are you really prepared to meet Him around the next curve in the road, or just over the next hill?

Sometimes, I think we seriously understate the fear factor when we speak of God with those who do not know Him. They are not prepared to meet Him, and the very thought of meeting Him should send them into bouts of soul-cleansing terror. The writer of the book of Hebrews reminds us that *"it is a dreadful thing to fall into the hands of the living God"* (Hebrews 10:31). I believe intuitively that in many instances the ungodly understand this truth better than believers do. When was the last time you heard a soul-stirring message on the fear of the LORD? We prefer our God to be soft and cuddly, so we have defanged and de-clawed the Lion of the Tribe of Judah. We have relegated the God of fearful judgment to those unread pages of the Old Testament. Surely, we reason, God has reformed His ways.

But my God is still an awesome God. I have carefully avoided using the word *awesome* to describe the Almighty up to this point. I have avoided the word because it is over-used and has lost its power. In its original form, the word *awesome* connotes a confrontation—an encounter—with knee-buckling, soul-arresting, pant-wetting consequences. Awesome? Our God is not awesome. He is uber-awesome. No human language can begin to capture the vast and fearful awesomeness of this holy God.

Yet it is this fear-inducing God we are to seek. Why seek after a lesser god? We are commanded to search for Him while He may be found. But why would we want to find this God, a God of holiness and judgment? How can we even coexist with this uber-awesome God?

We must seek and find Him so we can be forgiven. That is the only way we can cohabit the same neck of the woods. Remember that though this God is hidden, He always knows our exact whereabouts, and He can pounce upon us in love or in judgment at any moment He chooses. David knew he needed to find Him so he could be forgiven. I need His forgiveness too. I need this all-powerful, holy God on my side. I do not want to meet Him in judgment around the next bend. But rather, I need to find God so I can be reconciled to Him. Then I will discover that this hidden God is working behind the scenes on my behalf.

In 1 Chronicles we read of David celebrating the arrival of the Ark of the Covenant in Jerusalem by teaching Asaph and his priestly associates a psalm. In that psalm, David calls on the people of Israel to *"look to the LORD and his strength; seek his face always"* (1 Chronicles 16:11).

When in humility I call out to the strong One and find Him, I want His strength working with me, in me, and on my behalf.

About five hundred years after David taught the words to the above-mentioned psalm, the idolatrous people of Judah went into exile. After a long siege, Jerusalem was sacked and burned. The temple of the LORD was destroyed. Jeremiah, the weeping prophet, was charged with delivering God's stark message of judgment to the people of that time.

What I find most remarkable about this grievous time of judgment is God's command to Jeremiah. He is ordered by the LORD not to pray for the people of his homeland: *"Do not pray for this people nor offer any plea or petition for them, because I will not listen when they call to me in the time of their distress"* (Jeremiah 11:14).

In effect, God was saying that this was one of those times when He would be hidden from His people. He would not hear their prayers. They may seek after the LORD, but He would not be found. Though they cry out, the heavens would be as brass. Though I wish it were otherwise, there are times when God simply cannot be found. We read the Word of God and it is as dry and palatable as sawdust on our tongues. Our prayers fall to the ground lifeless, like so much deadwood and, though we wait, no answer comes.

Fortunately, seasons change. The cold winter of the soul does not last forever. Later, speaking of a time yet to come, Jeremiah reports,

> *Then you will call upon me and come to pray to me, and I will listen to you. You will seek me and find me when you seek me with all your heart. I will be found by you,' declares the LORD, 'and will bring you back from captivity* (Jeremiah 29:12–14).

The lesson we can draw from all this is that we should never presume that God is standing by to do our beckoning. He reveals himself to us when and as He sees fit. One believer may hear the audible voice of God while another can hear of God only through someone else. To one believer, God's Word is a feast of unmatched proportions, while another may struggle to glean even a single kernel from His Word. One believer hears the wondrous love of God being trumpeted straight into his heart; another questions if God even cares. Strangely, on the road of life these believers may find their roles completely reversed tomorrow. One who was so full of faith may be suddenly racked with doubt; another who was so close may become estranged. If we have seen His face today, we cannot presume the hidden God will be showing us His face tomorrow. We must rejoice in what He has revealed of Himself today and hold fast, for we do not know what tomorrow brings.

So let's heed David as he admonishes us, "*Let everyone who is godly pray to you, while you may be found.*"

If we have found the LORD, been forgiven by Him, and reconciled to Him, then we can build our lives on that Rock which is Christ. We can experience the security of the next statement David makes in this psalm: "*Surely when the mighty waters rise, they will not reach him. You are my hiding place; you will protect me from trouble and surround me with songs of deliverance.*"

The Rock, Christ, stands above all else. There is no higher ground. He towers above the storms of life, immovable and secure. Surely Jesus had this very passage in mind when He told the parable of the wise and foolish builders found in Matthew chapter seven. If we put Christ's teaching into practice, we have a foundation set upon that high Rock. Though the storm winds blow, the rains beat down, and the flood streams rise, "*they will not reach him.*" And the destructive force of the mighty waters will not reach us either, if our life is built on Him.

At times of catastrophe, we can find rest in this hiding place. Noah knew that hiding place during the greatest calamity to hit this planet. He also built his house, the ark, upon the Rock. When the rains began, it was the LORD who closed the door, shutting him in. While all outside perished, Noah and his family were hidden in God.

In the greatest storm to hit Europe during the twentieth century, a young Dutch woman found a hiding place in God. While Nazi terror reigned, Corrie ten Boom found refuge in the words of this psalm. Amid the horror of the concentration camp, she found a secret place, a hiding place secure from the raging storm.[3]

The LORD becomes our hiding place. Take a moment to imagine that. The uber-awesome, hidden God becomes our hiding place. I am tucked snugly between the paws of the great and fearsome Lion of the Tribe of Judah. None can harm me there. No cougar, no wild beast, no human scheme, no demon from hell can snatch me from between those fearsome, gentle paws. And while the storm rages, while the demons gnash their teeth, while kingdoms fall, I can hear the Lion's purr. He is protecting me from trouble. He is surrounding me with songs of deliverance.

Bringing Life to the Psalms

1. Have you read any of the books in the Chronicles of Narnia series by C.S. Lewis? Aslan, the great lion in the series, represents Christ, our redeeming King. Consider reading *The Lion, the Witch, and the Wardrobe*, or rent the movie. Be prepared for a blessing as you draw the links between this children's story and the great truths of the Gospel message.

2. What are you doing to seek God? This week, take special note of how God reveals Himself to you. Watch for Him. If we are not careful, we can miss the ways He manifests His presence in our lives. A journal can be helpful way to record these events.

3. We all need a shelter from the storms of life. Are you going through a difficult time right now? Throw yourself into the arms of Jesus. He knows how to shelter you.

----

[3] *The Hiding Place* by Corrie ten Boom, Random House, Inc., 1982, paperback.

4. The God we seek also revealed Himself as the Savior—the predator God—who actively seeks us. Jesus said, *"The Son of Man came to seek and to save what was lost"* (Luke 19:10). Take a moment to read the account of how Jesus pounced on Zacchaeus, the tree-sitting tax collector. Jesus is a hunter, hunting sinners that he might save them. Read Luke 19:1–10 to catch a glimpse of the Lion of the Tribe of Judah on the prowl.

The LORD Speaks

*I will instruct you and teach you
in the way you should go;
I will counsel you and watch over you.
Do not be like the horse or the mule,
which have no understanding
but must be controlled by bit and bridle
or they will not come to you.
Many are the woes of the wicked,
but the LORD's unfailing love
surrounds the man who trusts in him.
Rejoice in the LORD and be glad, you righteous;
sing, all you who are upright in heart!*

ON A RECENT SUNDAY MORNING
I spent an hour and a half at a local university radio station. I was
there as a special guest on the station's weekly contemporary gospel
music program. The host of the show introduced me, and between

various music selections we engaged in some lively banter. I talked about the books I have written, and I did a number of spoken word dramatizations of the Bible. This was live radio. Throughout the on-air time, both the host and I needed to be verbally on our toes, always ready to jump in at a moment's notice. The greatest fear of any radio host is "dead air," that awkward silence that indicates someone has missed their verbal cue. That noise box that we call the radio must always be pumping out music, advertisements, or conversation. Silence is the great taboo of any broadcast medium. To connect to the listeners, the audio broadcaster must never go silent.

Prayer, however, works differently. It has been said that prayer is a two-way street. To put it another way, God answers back when we pray. Consequently, during times of prayer we need to listen for God instead of only speaking out our requests. True prayer is two-way communication.

Unfortunately, this kind of prayer is only rarely modeled during times of public worship. Think for a moment of what might happen if the pastor or worship leader at your church led the congregation in prayer and then paused to say, "Now let's wait for God to answer."

Silence might well follow. The listeners in the congregation might experience some "dead air." We have been conditioned to see this as somehow wrong. We immediately feel that someone has missed their cue; they have dropped the ball. Every moment during a church service must be filled with music or audible verbal communication of some kind. Like the radio broadcaster, we have come to regard silence as a taboo, as though it were our enemy. But in that silence, if we are listening, God might speak.

Perhaps public prayer as we know it is not prayer at all. In most cases it is only one-way communication. If that is so, we may more closely resemble the Pharisee about whom Jesus warned us in the Gospel of Luke, and the resemblance may be greater than we even dared imagine. In the parable of the tax collector and the Pharisee, we are told that, "*the Pharisee stood and prayed to himself*" (Luke 18:11).

Every minister of the gospel should ask him or herself, "When I pray in public, am I like the Pharisee, praying to myself? Am I praying just to be heard by my audience? Am I praying to the LORD or am I posturing for people? Am I effectively modeling that prayer is two-way communication? How do I allow God to speak back to the congregation?"

In Psalm 32, God speaks back. David begins this psalm and we can clearly hear his voice addressing us as he tells how wonderful it is to be forgiven. He then goes on to speak of his own struggle with unconfessed sin. Finally, he tells us of the great relief he experienced as he is pardoned and restored to a place of close fellowship with the LORD. But then abruptly in verse eight we hear a different voice. God is speaking. The LORD responds to what David has said. This psalm is two-way communication.

We have heard David's words; let's hear God's words now. "*I will instruct you and teach you in the way you should go; I will counsel you and watch over you.*"

Clearly this is not David's voice. David is not going to counsel and watch over us. This is the work of the LORD. It is the LORD who will teach and guide us. It is His role to shepherd the flock of His pasture.

These words, from verse eight to the end of this psalm, are coming from the LORD. David has heard God speak and now he is passing on this message from the LORD directly to us. In this respect, David is fulfilling the role of a prophet. He is acting as God's spokesperson. In fact, in Acts 2:29–30, Peter asserts that David was a prophet. And what is a prophet? In the simplest terms, it is someone who hears God, and then passes on God's message to others.

Do you hear God? This is no idle, rhetorical question. It is essential to our Christian faith that we as believers hear the voice of God.

I would go so far as to say that you cannot experience salvation unless you first hear God. Jesus said, *"My sheep listen to my voice; I know them, and they follow me. I give them eternal life, and they shall never perish"* (John 10:27–28).

In short, we must be able to hear Jesus in order to follow Him, and it is in following Him that we receive eternal life.

At this point, in my mind's eye, I can see some of my readers furrowing their brows with worry. They are asking, "Do I really hear God's voice?"

In all likelihood the answer is a resounding, "Yes, you hear God's voice."

If you have felt the convicting power of the Holy Spirit revealing your sin to you, then you have heard God. If you have taken those sins to God in prayer, then you have obeyed the voice of God. If you have felt joy in knowing that your sins are forgiven, then in your spirit you have heard the Good Shepherd's pardon. Rejoice then, because you have heard His voice and are part of His flock.

Within the context of Psalm 32, we have seen all of this play out in the life of David. He has been convicted of sin, he has confessed his sin, and he has received God's pardoning forgiveness. Because of all this he is numbered among the blessed, even as he states at the beginning of this psalm: *"Blessed is he whose transgressions are forgiven, whose sins are covered."*

If you have heard and obeyed God's voice, you too are among that blessed number. We are assured by the LORD in the words of this psalm: *"I will instruct you and teach you in the way you should go."*

Now this is a promise you can hang your hat on. If you have your ears open to hear the LORD, you can be sure that He will speak into your life to provide guidance. Remember, our God is a God of infinite variety. He can speak to you in numerous ways. Here are some of them:

The LORD Speaks

God can speak to you and direct you

- through the holy Scriptures

- through the gentle nudge of the Holy Spirit

- through his anointed servant leaders

- through events and circumstances

- through open doors and closed doors

- through dreams and visions

- through prophetic words

- even through the words of the ungodly.

Please bear in mind that this is intended only as an illustrative list, not an exhaustive list. If you have come to Christ, the Good Shepherd, you can rest assured that He *"will instruct you and teach you in the way you should go."*

Many years ago now, a teaching colleague suggested I take a summer university course in a subject I particularly enjoyed but in which I had no formal training. Taking the course meant leaving my young family for a full month in the summer, taking a temporary leave from my pastoral responsibilities, and finding a temporary residence in a city five hours away. I also needed to come up with money I did not have to pay for tuition and all the other related expenses. Furthermore, taking this course came with no guarantee that a teaching position would be waiting for me at the end of the process. Though I mentioned this suggested course to my wife, we both dismissed the idea as impractical and unworkable in our circumstances. I gave it no further thought.

One night about two weeks later, I went to bed as usual and promptly fell asleep. About an hour later I was abruptly aroused from a deep sleep by a voice saying, "You need to take that course."

I was so startled by this voice that I was breathless for several seconds. My wife was sound asleep beside me. It was clear that she had not spoken; this voice did not sound at all like hers. It was a different, yet somehow familiar voice.

Then I was reminded of the story of the young boy Samuel, who was called out of his place of sleep by the LORD. The full account can be found in 1 Samuel 3. I could only conclude that the LORD was calling me out of a dead sleep to set me on a course of action I had earlier rejected. I resolved right then to obey the midnight voice.

That decision set into motion a whole series of events which, when taken together, can only be described as miraculous. Money arrived from unexpected sources. Doors opened that had previously been shut. An unknown relative offered lodging in the city where the course was offered. And most surprising of all, within days of saying yes to the voice, through a series of divinely arranged coincidences, I was hired for a teaching position based on my decision to take that summer course. When I said yes to the LORD, He went before me and prepared the way.

Through this entire experience I was learning the truth of the words, *"I will instruct you and teach you in the way you should go; I will counsel you and watch over you."*

Are you about to make a choice that will affect the course of your entire life? Take that decision to the LORD. Do not make that decision by yourself. Pray with a listening heart. Here in His word, we have His promise. The LORD *"will instruct you and teach you in the way you should go; [He] will counsel you and watch over you."*

When you set your feet on the course God has chosen for you, He will watch over you. There is ongoing counsel as you walk on the path that He has chosen for you. Listen for it. It can come in a variety of ways, including a voice at midnight.

By way of contrast, we read this admonition from the LORD: *"Do not be like the horse or the mule, which have no understanding but* must be controlled by bit and bridle or they will not come to you."

For those unfamiliar with a horse's bit and bridle, this metaphor may require some explanation. The bit and bridle are really the steering mechanisms for the horse and rider. The bit is a round metal bar attached to the bridle. It is inserted into the horse's mouth. A slight pull on both reins should bring the horse to a stop. A tug on the right rein will direct the horse to the right, and of course a tug on the left rein turns the horse to the left. The bit works because it pulls on the soft lips of the horse. A stubborn horse can seize control by clamping the bit in his teeth, leaving the rider powerless to provide direction.

My father grew up working with horses. He once had a horse that habitually took the bit in its teeth whenever the time for an unpleasant task arrived. The horse seized control for that moment, but in reality he was setting himself on a direct route to the dog food factory. As a work horse he was useless, unreliable, and, when needed most, he was out of control.

If we refuse to hear what God is saying to us, we are like that horse. We are taking our own direction, setting out on the wrong path—a path that leads to destruction.

Lest we miss the point, the LORD has both a warning and an encouragement for us. "Many are the woes of the wicked, but the LORD's unfailing love surrounds the man who trusts in him."

The choice before us is clear. If we heed the LORD's call, He surrounds us with His unfailing love. Oh, what a promise! If we choose to listen to another voice and follow the wrong path, a life of woe will follow. We need to choose our path carefully. What do you want to be surrounded by—the LORD's love or self-inflicted woe?

If we trust and obey, we embark on a course that will bring us lasting joy—joy down to the core, spilling over the sides, and filling our days. And the LORD has some final instructions for us if we have heard Him and embarked on that course: "Rejoice in the LORD and be glad, you righteous; sing all you who are upright in heart!"

Bringing Life to the Psalms

1. Read the calling of Samuel found in 1 Samuel 3. Have you ever felt God was calling you to a particular course of action? How did you respond?

2. Are you currently facing choices that will affect the direction of your life? Take time to pray and wait for God to answer. Have others pray with you as well. Close friends who also walk with the LORD can provide wise counsel and confirm God's will for your life.

3. If you are walking on God's chosen path for your life, take some time to rejoice. Give Him thanks for leading you so clearly. Sing and let your worship flow to the LORD.

4. Reread Psalm 32. Take time to listen as you read. What is God saying to you by His Spirit?

An Ever-Present Help

Of the Sons of Korah

God is our refuge and strength,
an ever-present help in trouble.
Therefore we will not fear,
though the earth give way
and the mountains fall into the heart of the sea,
though its waters roar and foam
and the mountains quake with their surging.
(Selah)
There is a river whose streams make glad the
city of God,
the holy place where the Most High dwells.
God is within her, she will not fall;
God will help her at break of day.

WHERE WERE YOU ON
September 11, 2001? What were you doing when you heard the
news of the horrific attacks on the World Trade Center and the
Pentagon? I was at school at the time, on a break between classes.

The equipment repairman had just arrived to fix some of the power tools in the woodworking shop. He seemed rather agitated as he reported, "A plane has hit the World Trade Center in New York."

I was unfazed by this news and responded, "It's probably just a small two-passenger plane. What's the big deal?"

"No. It was a big passenger jet," the repairman said with a shake of his head. This made no sense to me, and with that said, the repairman returned to his truck, where he sat for a minute or two listening to the vehicle's radio.

He returned in an even more animated state to report, "A second plane has crashed into the other tower."

At this point I turned on the classroom radio and began listening to the reports myself. The true emotional impact of these events did not hit me, however, until about an hour later. On a classroom television that was hastily moved into the school custodian's office, I watched the towers come crashing to the ground. My whole body was left shaking.

Now, years later, the whole earth is still reverberating from the impact of those events.

At church gatherings, when I do live spoken-word dramatizations of the fourteen psalms that form the basis for this book, I can no longer perform Psalm 46 without evoking memories of the day we call 9/11. Instantly, the pictures of the planes hitting the towers flash into my mind. Once again the towers disintegrate and come crashing down onto the streets, onto the people and rescue workers below.

Psalm 46 begins with these words: *"God is our refuge and strength, an ever-present help in trouble. Therefore we will not fear, though the earth give way."*

The earth gave way on September 11, 2001. If the earth falls out from under you—if everything you have known to be secure suddenly disintegrates—how can you not succumb to fear? Fear is a person's natural response to such events. If the earth gives way beneath us, then the only One we have to hold onto is God. If all earthly securities disintegrate, the only remaining refuge is our heavenly Father.

I dare say that too many North American Christians know God only as a God of sunny days, full bellies, and prosperity. I would place myself in that category. For most of us personally, the earth has not fallen away from beneath us. What will become of us when it does? Are we even remotely prepared for such events? Can we ever be fully prepared? Are you ready for the hundred-story plunge to the street below?

Against this backdrop, for all to hear, the psalmist declares,

> *God is our refuge and strength, an ever-present help in trouble. Therefore we will not fear, though the earth give way and the mountains fall into the heart of the sea, though its waters roar and foam and the mountains quake with their surging.*

On December 26, 2004, at 7:58:53 a.m. local time, the mountains beneath the sea off the coast of the Indonesian island of Sumatra began to quake. The earthquake registered a magnitude 9.2 on the Richter scale, making it the second most powerful earthquake ever recorded. It also was the longest earthquake in duration. This devastating temblor unleashed a tsunami that claimed the lives of an estimated 229,866 people. The ocean surge reached a height of 30 meters (100 feet) in places, and it killed people as distant as 8,000 kilometers (5,000 miles) from the epicenter.

Since that date, I cannot perform Psalm 46 without evoking memories of the Boxing Day tsunami. Instantly the pictures of walls of water come flooding into my mind. Once again, whole villages were scoured off the coast like so much worthless refuse that is swept out to sea. Men, women, and children disappeared in a muddy seething swill of saltwater debris.

But despite all this—in the midst of all this, as though he had been granted a preview of this very event—the psalmist says, *"God is our refuge and strength, an ever-present help in trouble. Therefore we will not fear, though the earth give way and the mountains fall into the heart of the sea, though its waters roar and foam and the mountains quake with their surging."*

From this scene of utter devastation the psalmist transitions to the polar opposite. He brings us to the Gates of Splendor, and within those gates we find *"there is a river whose streams make glad the city of God, the holy place where the Most High dwells. God is within her, she will not fall; God will help her at break of day."*

What a contrast! Here is our place of refuge. Here in that holy place, we are face to face with God, the God who is our strength. We are at the source point of gladness. There is an endless supply of the water of life within this sacred city. The Master calls, "Come and drink."

Are you drinking even now?

How can we face an uncertain future without fear when the world around us is being torn apart? That question is really the primary focus of this psalm. Here beside the river of God we can find the answer.

Lloyd Ogilvie in his book, *Facing the Future without Fear*[4], points out that God's most frequently repeated command in the Scriptures is, "Fear not."

We are not to fear men, circumstances, or the demons of hell. We are not to fret or worry. After all, worry is simply a case of borrowing fear from the Bank of Insecurity in order to make a down payment on a future event that, despite our worries, is unlikely to occur. That truly is an unwise investment. Ogilvie points out that in the Bible there are 366 commands for us not to fear, one for every day of the year, including one for leap year. In short, God's Word for us daily is, "Fear not!"

---

[4] *Facing the Future Without Fear: Prescriptions for Courageous Living in the New Millennium* (paperback) by Lloyd J. Ogilvie, Vine Books, 2002 edition.

Why is our ability to overcome fear so important to God? Could it be that God sees that fear imprisons us? It prevents us from doing God's will for our lives. Fear locks us into patterns of behavior that keep us from growing and maturing in our faith. If we are afraid of what others think, we will never share our faith. If we are afraid to risk going without, we will never know the full joy of true giving. If we fear rejection, we will never risk opening our hearts to love. If we play it safe and, like a turtle, keep our heads in our shells, we will never truly experience life to the full.

On a stormy night, Peter stepped out of a boat in the middle of a lake and walked on the water. Think of it. What a perfectly insane thing to do! He rejected fear and chose Jesus. Jesus called him out of that boat. He said, *"Come"* (Matthew 14:29).

You can do what Peter did only if you know the One who is calling you. Peter knew Jesus. He recognized His call and stepped out of natural security (the boat) into the supernatural security of Christ's call. He walked by faith, a faith that transcended what is seen and reached into the heavenly realm, *"the holy place where the Most High dwells."*

Psalm 46 calls us to life on that higher plane. We can overcome fear if we have tasted the waters of those streams that make glad the city of God. This is the same living water that Jesus offered to the woman at the well (see John 4). In the midst of the storms of life, the psalmist invites us to come to that higher plane. He calls us aside. In times of trouble he invites us to embrace our citizenship in the city of God.

How can we face an uncertain future without fear? If you have died to the elemental passions of this world, you can live your life beyond fear and worry. Dead men do not panic. The apostle Paul urged the Colossian believers to acknowledge their death to this world and embrace their new life in Christ: *"Set your minds on things above, not on earthly things. For you died, and your life is now hidden with Christ in God"* (Colossians 3:2–3).

Repeatedly in his epistles, Paul likens baptism to death, burial, and resurrection. This is our point of identification with Christ as we begin a new life of faith in Him. And a life of faith is precisely to what we are called to as believers in our resurrected Lord, who has ascended to the heavenly Jerusalem before us. That life of faith triumphs over fear. It turns defeat into conquest, doubt into certainty, death into the ultimate victory.

My own hunger for a deeper knowledge of the Psalms was sparked by a middle-aged couple, John and Clare Tremblay. The Tremblays had attended our church for a few years, but then they moved to another part of the city and we lost touch. Upon their return to our neighborhood, we discovered that Clare had developed diabetes and had gone blind. I began to make regular pastoral visits to their home. On these visits it became my habit to read a psalm to Clare, while John stood nearby. She drew such strength and comfort from these psalms; you could see her face light up every time a psalm was read. Unfortunately, her condition deteriorated rapidly. After a number of falls, it became clear that she was unable to walk. Soon she was confined to a long-term care facility. Even there she found her refuge in the Psalms. It seemed to be the only thing that could put a smile on her face.

You see, for that moment Clare was no longer blind. She could see, and she was sitting by the *"river whose streams make glad the city of God, the holy place where the Most High dwells."* While she listened to the Psalms, her mind was set on things above where her life was hidden with Christ in God. Within those psalms she found God—the God who is an ever-present help in time of trouble.

As time went by, I could see in Clare the truth of the words, *"God is within her, she will not fall; God will help her at break of day."*

One morning Clare found herself there, in the very presence of the LORD. This psalm had become her reality. Her funeral became a celebration of the psalms she loved, and the God of refuge that she found within those psalms.

After Clare's passing I paid a number of visits to John to offer some comfort and support to him as he mourned the loss of his wife. "Pastor, could you read me a psalm?" John asked.

Of course I brought my Bible along to do just that. He sat in rapt attention as I read. He got that wistful, far-off look in his eyes, and I knew where he was. He was crouched by one of those streams that make glad the city of God. He was having a good, thirst-quenching drink.

On one of those visits John complained of a backache, and I suggested he have a doctor check it. A few weeks later John's daughter-in-law called. John was in the hospital. The backache was spinal cancer, and the doctors said that John had only a month to live. In fact, he lasted only three weeks. John was on a three-week, hundred-story plunge to death—a plunge he faced without a hint of fear.

I recall those hospital visits. They were tinged with bittersweet warmth. John had watched his bride of forty years face death with faith and courage. Now he did the same. Through a fog of pain John would smile up at me, and in a hoarse whisper he would say, "Pastor, could you read me a psalm?"

On my last visit with John, I read Psalm 46. I cleared my throat and began, "*God is our refuge and strength, an ever-present help in trouble. Therefore we will not fear, though the earth give way*"

John smiled his biggest smile. He knew the truth of those words even as the earth beneath him was giving way.

John and Clare were both in their early sixties. They died within six months of each other. In me they sparked an ongoing love for the Book of Psalms. It's a love that I trust will carry me into eternity even as it carried them, because I know, "*there is a river whose streams make glad the city of God, the holy place where the Most High dwells.*"

Bringing Life to the Psalms

1. Read the account of Peter and Jesus walking on the water found in Matthew 14:22–36. Consider what this story says to you about walking with Jesus. What does it say to you about faith and fear? Is Jesus calling you to a walk of faith? Is he calling you out of your comfort zone?

2. What do you think Paul means when he says, "*Set your minds on things above, not on earthly things. For you died, and your life is now hidden with Christ in God*" (Colossians 3:2–3)? How can you live your life simultaneously here on earth and in heaven with Christ? Setting your mind takes personal discipline. It involves purposeful thought. What godly disciplines help you to set your mind on things above?

3. Has God been a God of sunny days and prosperity for you? Praise God for all the good times. Have you also faced adversity and trouble as you walked with the Lord? How did your faith help you overcome?

Be Still and Know that I am God

Nations are in uproar, kingdoms fall;
he lifts his voice, the earth melts.
The LORD Almighty is with us;
the God of Jacob is our fortress. (Selah)
Come and see the works of the LORD,
the desolations he has brought on the earth.
He makes wars cease to the ends of the earth;
he breaks the bow and shatters the spear,
he burns the shields with fire.
"Be still, and know that I am God;
I will be exalted among the nations,
I will be exalted in the earth."
The LORD Almighty is with us;
the God of Jacob is our fortress. (Selah)

PERHAPS NO OTHER PSALM CAP-
tures the essence of the cataclysmic as completely as Psalm 46. Here
with the psalmist we catch a glimpse of the apocalypse. The world of
this psalm is in utter turmoil. It quakes. It writhes. It melts. Through

a poetic eye we are viewing the death throes of a planet.

I spent New Years Day, 1985, in Hiroshima, Japan—a city well acquainted with cataclysm. Today, Hiroshima is a beautiful city. It is a seaside city built on a flat river delta, surrounded by mountains. Seven river channels cut across the city's fertile flood plain on their way to the blue waters of Hiroshima Bay. In many respects, Hiroshima resembles a more compact, oriental version of Vancouver.

But on August 6, 1945, this beautiful city became a terrestrial picture of hell. The horrors inflicted on Hiroshima are without parallel in human history. In an atomic flash, 66,000 residents were instantly killed. They were the fortunate ones. Another 60,000 died later of their injuries or from the effects of radiation sickness. The accounts of their suffering are among the most heart- wrenching literature I have ever read.

I was not in Hiroshima alone; my wife and my two-and-a-half-year-old son were with me. Together on a cool but sunny New Years Day, we strolled through the Hiroshima Peace Memorial Park. We slowly walked around the building known as the A-Bomb Dome. This devastated stone structure was the only building left standing after the atomic blast. Its skeletal structure is a visible reminder of that grim day in 1945. Is this stark ruin also a portent of our future and the future of our planet?

Across the ages the psalmist speaks, "*Nations are in uproar, kingdoms fall; He lifts his voice, the earth melts.*"

In 1945, the nations of the world were in uproar and kingdoms were falling. In Europe, the vaunted thousand-year rule of the Third Reich came to a brutal end. Great cities lay in ruins. Millions were exterminated; millions more were displaced and starving. A demon in human flesh had put the whole apparatus of the modern state to work to eradicate God's people. The last victim of every murderous demon is its human host, so staying true to Satanic form, in the final days of war, Hitler and his leading Nazi henchmen pulled the trigger on their own demise.

Across the Pacific, expansionist, Imperial Japan was on the verge of collapse. The emperor, whose subjects worshipped him as a god, was about to call an end to a war that was cannibalizing his own people. Emperor Hirohito was revered as a descendant of the sun god, and through brutal military conquest the land of the Rising Sun had spread its rays across much of Asia. But before the emperor could call a halt to the war, a different kind of sun would ignite a blazing inferno in the heart of the nation.

Nuclear physicists will tell you that in its simplest form, an atomic bomb is the power of the sun released upon the earth. The heat and radiation are of the same magnitude. A miniature sun flashed 100 million volts of raw energy over Hiroshima at 8:15 a.m. on August 6, 1945.

People beneath the epicentre of the blast were simply vaporised. Later that day in the Atomic Bomb Museum, my eyes bore witness to this phenomenon. Dark shadows were all that remained of men who were sitting on the stone steps of a bank building. Their bodies left something resembling a photographic imprint on the stone. In an instant – in a flash – they were gone.

Miles from the epicenter, brass globes drooped and melted on the side facing this new sun that had come to the earth. The effects of the intense heat of the nuclear flash upon human flesh can only be imagined. On many survivors, clothing and skin exposed just for an instant simply melted away.

Again across the ages the psalmist speaks, "*Nations are in uproar, kingdoms fall; He lifts his voice, the earth melts.*"

You view all these things in a different light when you are with your family. My wife was walking beside me on this tour. She was into her third month of pregnancy. I was either carrying my two-year-old son in my arms, holding his little hand, or pushing him in a stroller. I kept asking myself, "What kind of world am I bringing my children into? Will they experience these things—this hell—in their lifetimes?"

Today's newspaper headlines are not reassuring. More than twenty years have passed since my visit to Hiroshima, and thus far the world has avoided nuclear holocaust. But once again we appear to be creeping closer to the brink of annihilation. I began writing this chapter two days ago, and in one of those odd cases of divine coincidence, when I retrieved my morning newspaper from its slot in the screen door today, the headline read, "North Korea Conducts Nuclear Test."

If a rogue state like North Korea does not raise the level of our concern, we can always look to Iran and its nuclear ambitions. Meanwhile, Russia is edging ever closer toward a return to dictatorship. Then there is China, which is growing more powerful and restive as its economic might increases. In short, we live in a very dangerous and unpredictable world.

If newspaper headlines are not reassuring, Bible prophecies are even less so. The apostle Peter, speaking nearly a thousand years after Psalm 46 was penned, states, "*the present heavens and earth are reserved for fire, being kept for the day of judgment and destruction of ungodly men*" (2 Peter 3:7).

Peter goes on to evoke the very images of Psalm 46.

> *The day of the Lord will come like a thief. The heavens will disappear with a roar; the elements will be destroyed by fire, and the earth and everything in it will be laid bare* (2 Peter 3:10).

But over this inferno—this world afire—the psalmist speaks: "*The* LORD *Almighty is with us; the God of Jacob is our fortress.*"

We will not face this worldwide conflagration alone. We are not abandoned. The LORD has not left our side. We are not to yield to fear and worry. Though the ungodly perish, we have these words of assurance: "*The* LORD *Almighty is with us; the God of Jacob is our fortress.*" If we must face dark days, we will not face them alone. We will face them with the LORD Almighty.

There are many names for God, and good poetry is all about the choice of words. It is significant to note that the psalmist chose the particular name combination "*the* LORD *Almighty*" at this juncture in this psalm. The LORD, which is the Hebrew translation of Yahweh or Jehovah, means I AM. The great I AM is with us. The God of the burning bush has come to be with us. It is this God, who told Moses, "*I* AM *who I* AM" (Exodus 3:14). He will carry us through this time of apocalyptic turmoil. And not only is I AM, the self-existent One, with us, the psalmist also asserts that this great I AM is none other than the Almighty. In cataclysm we will see the power of the Almighty. He not only holds the power to melt the world and its elements with a fervent heat, he also has the power to save and deliver his own from that cataclysmic destruction if he so chooses.

Shadrach, Meshach, and Abednego walked out of the blazing furnace unscathed because the Almighty was with them (Daniel 3). In Psalm 46 we are assured that this same God, the LORD Almighty, will be with us. He will be with us when the end-times, world-consuming conflagration hits. The Almighty will be standing there in the furnace with us. His invisible mantle of protection will be extended over us, because "*the God of Jacob is our fortress.*"

By invoking the name of the God of Jacob, the psalmist links us to the great redemptive history of God's people. This is the God who saves, who intervenes in the affairs of men. He is the God who brought Jacob back safely to the land of promise after years of foreign sojourn. He is the God who visited Egypt with the ten plagues but, by the blood of a lamb, set apart His own people and so saved them from the Angel of Death. It was the God of Jacob who parted the Red Sea for His people, but destroyed the pursuing army. He is the God who destroyed the world in the great flood, but who floated His eight-person restoration mission over the top of the billowing torrent. In these and a thousand other biblical stories, He is a God who saves. He is a fortress round about those who call on His name. In the fortress we rest secure, no matter what fiery maelstrom should assault.

Throughout history, God's people have found safety and refuge in the fortress. Martin Luther knew all too well the assaults of hell. It was from within the fortress that he took his stand against the legions of hell. He would not bow to error even under the threat of death. He stood upon the unchanging, inerrant Word of God. When he left the Diet of Worms, he was a marked man—marked for execution. But even then he was safe. He was safe because a fortress surrounded him and protected him wherever he travelled. You see, Luther's fortress was the God of Jacob. How fitting then, that in addition to translating the whole Bible, he should pen the words to that great hymn, *"A Mighty Fortress is our God."*

Now the psalmist beckons us closer. *"Come and see the works of the LORD, the desolations he has brought on the earth. He makes wars to cease to the ends of the earth. He breaks the bow and shatters the spear; he burns the shields with fire."*

We live in a world that denies the existence of God, or at best sees God as aloof and distant from the historical events that shape societies and the course of nations. But is this an accurate world view? The Old Testament writers had a completely different perspective. They saw God as active in the affairs of men. He does not stand aloof from His creation, but rather He is the great Conductor of History. Nations move at His impulse. He raises up one kingdom and sets down another. At His discretion, He exalts one leader and humiliates another.

Reading the above passage from the Psalms can be quite disturbing to some of us. It disturbs me. Does God really bring desolation on the earth? Does he take sides in war? We may prefer our God to be more passive and distant. Perhaps God is a pacifist? He certainly loves peace. Yet in the Bible, God actively intervened in great battles and wars. And sometimes, to the consternation of God's people, He was helping the other side. The LORD used heathen Babylon to bring divine judgment down upon Judah.

Has God changed? Perhaps He has reformed in his old age? What would a twentieth century history text look like if it was written by Nehemiah, Isaiah, or Jeremiah? Would Isaiah see God's hand of judgment being unleashed on Nazi Germany? Was God actively working against this murderer of millions with his hell-hatched theory of racial supremacy? Was the God of the heavens ready to share His glory with the earthbound emperor of Japan? Did the LORD sanction the sun god's conquest of Asia, or did the Creator of the universe have the final say on the matter? Were the master theorists behind atheistic communism correct, or did the LORD laugh at them in derision? Did the Soviet empire collapse under its own weight, or was the LORD helping a few Polish believers as they pulled the last few bricks out of the crumbling foundation?

No nation can gloat in a state of moral superiority. The stench of sin hovers over the whole globe. Is this world ripe for God's judgment? Are we facing apocalypse over the next horizon?

Into global chaos the LORD speaks, *"Be still, and know that I am God; I will be exalted among the nations, I will be exalted in the earth."* From start to finish, this psalm evokes a thousand images of catastrophe, but it is the last picture that should lodge most deeply in our hearts. It is the picture of a hurt young child rushing home into the arms of a loving parent. The world has hurt us. But in these arms we will find love, healing, and courage to face the world, and to face a new day. At the core, where it counts most, we are loved by our Father. Over that frightened, wounded child our Father speaks the words, *"Be still, and know that I am God; I will be exalted among the nations, I will be exalted in the earth."*

I need to hear those words spoken to me. In the rush of life I need to pause. I need to stop and hear God as I'm curled up in His arms. When pain and fear and worry come, He says, *"Be still."*

Quiet your heart in God. He is bigger than your problems—bigger than the whole cruel world out there. He is in control of world events. Yield to His control in your own life. He holds the future—your future—in His hands—and they are loving hands. Though nations are in uproar and kingdoms fall, His Kingdom stands secure and eternal. When you are still—still and at rest in His Kingdom—you know the truth of the words, *"The LORD Almighty is with us; the God of Jacob is our fortress."*

Bringing Life to the Psalms

1. Read the account of Shadrach, Meshach, and Abednego in the fiery furnace, as found in the third chapter of Daniel. Consider what this story says to you about facing persecution and calamity with courage.

2. Do you have a hymnal handy? Take time to read or sing, *"A Mighty Fortress is our God."* The lyrics are a powerful declaration of the supremacy of God in a world gone mad. You may also wish to view the movie, *"Luther."* It is an accurate portrayal of the faith and struggles of this courageous reformer.

3. End-times theology, or eschatology, is frequently a source of fear rather than comfort. Psalm 46 can act as a counterweight to many of the rather frightening passages found in the Book of Revelation. How can this psalm help you view the end-times in a more positive light?

4. As we conclude this look at Psalm 46, take a moment to reread this apocalyptic psalm. What is God saying to you by His Spirit?

The Harvest Psalm

*May God be gracious to us and bless us
and make his face shine upon us, (Selah)
that your ways may be known on earth,
your salvation among all nations.
May the peoples praise you, O God;
may all the peoples praise you.
May the nations be glad and sing for joy,
for you rule the peoples justly
and guide the nations of the earth. (Selah)
May the peoples praise you, O God;
may all the peoples praise you.
Then the land will yield its harvest,
and God, our God, will bless us.
God will bless us,
and all the ends of the earth will fear him.*

I AM GLAD THAT WE CELEBRATE
Thanksgiving in early October here in Canada. I cannot imagine
waiting until late November to celebrate this holiday as Americans
do. It puts Thanksgiving too close to Christmas, and it delays it too

long after the harvest has been gathered. By late November, harvest time is just a distant memory and much of the country is already in winter's icy grip. Thanksgiving is, after all, a harvest festival, signaling our thankfulness to God for the bounty of the earth.

When you grow up on a farm as I did, you appreciate the traditional aspects of Thanksgiving all the more. You are reminded each day that the food on your table does not simply come from a store. You are actively engaged in producing the nourishment that sustains your own life.

As a youngster I sat down to many a Thanksgiving feast, and almost all the food found on that groaning table was home grown. I watched those vegetables growing in our garden in the hot summer sun. I even pulled the weeds from around those peas. As for those mashed potatoes, I helped my mother hill those tubers in the spring and then dug them up after the frost hit in the fall. My brother loved growing pumpkins, and Mom would turn his favorite into the best pumpkin pie east of the Rockies. And how can you eat pumpkin pie without a mound of whipped cream on top? Well let me tell you, it tastes even better when just that morning you milked the cows that produce that sweet rich cream. Oh, and that huge turkey—we'll miss that pompous strutting gobbler out by the henhouse, but I'm sure we'll get over it, somehow. For now, let's just dig in.

Let's all dig in, and give thanks to the God who made all this possible. This sumptuous feast has been brought to you by Him. Now that's Thanksgiving!

The great God in heaven has been kind to us. He has answered our prayers. He brought the warmth of spring and the rain of heaven. He caused His face to shine upon us. The rich earth responded to his touch. It brought forth its bounty, and now around this table we have gathered together as a family to celebrate God's great goodness to us.

The opening petition of Psalm 67 has been granted. *"May God be gracious to us and bless us and make his face shine upon us, that your ways may be known on earth, your salvation among all nations."*

God has been gracious. We did not earn this blessing. Yes, we worked. We tilled the soil, we planted the seed. But it was God who brought the increase. He has blessed the work of our hands. He has smiled on our efforts and, during this feast, every mouth-watering bite testifies to his amazing love and goodness. Let's all dig in! *"Taste and see that the* LORD *is good"* (Psalm 34:8).

Have you ever asked yourself, why? Why is God so good? Why has he blessed us so richly? Why are His mercies new every morning? Why is He so forgiving? Why does He provide in such abundance?

The simple answer is because that is His nature. He is kind, so He loves to bless us whether we deserve it or not. He is loving, so His blessings flow like water flows down a mountainside. Can rivers flow uphill? That's impossible. In the same way, it is impossible for God not to be loving, gracious, and merciful. It is simply His nature to pour out blessings.

Like any loving parent, God draws pleasure from blessing His children. But is there a divine motivation that extends beyond the family of God? As the opening verse of this psalm makes clear, God desires to bless us so that His ways and His salvation may be known all over this world.

So then, Psalm 67 should be our prayer, not only for ourselves but for the world. *"May God be gracious to us and bless us and make his face shine upon us, that your ways may be known on earth, your salvation among all nations."*

In other words, God's blessing is not solely for us. It is to extend around the world and beyond the family of God. Is God in fact blessing us abundantly so that we may in turn bless others? Is He blessing us, so that we may make His salvation known among all nations? That certainly would appear to be the plan according to Psalm 67.

This is perhaps the most evangelical of all the psalms. By that I mean there is good news in this psalm, and the good news of God's loving-kindness found here is not to be kept to oneself. It is to be taken to the whole world.

In addition to an enormous feast, I have another childhood memory that is also linked to Thanksgiving. On Thanksgiving Sunday, as on every Sunday of the year, we would all dress up in our Sunday best and then squeeze into the family sedan for the four-mile (six-kilometer) trip to our local country church. For my mother, preparing the family brood of six children for church and then stuffing Grandma, Dad, six squirming kids, and herself into one car was no simple feat. I am sure that for her, stuffing a twenty-five-pound turkey was much easier and it was accomplished with far less stress.

On Sunday mornings, the last thing we did before leaving the house was to prepare our church offering. Everybody gave. Every child and every adult had their own offering envelope and typically, Dad gave each child a dollar to put in that envelope. At a time when a chocolate bar cost fifteen cents and I could get a heaping ice-cream cone for one thin dime, this was quite a princely sum. I suppose Dad could have combined all that money and put it all in one single envelope—his own. After all, every cent of it was actually his money. But he chose to distribute it to his children, for us to put into the offering basket. I can only suppose that he wanted to train each of us to be givers.

Thanksgiving Sunday, however, was different. On that Sunday, unlike all the others during the year, we did not get a dollar from Dad. This was harvest time; the crop had come in. God had been good and we were blessed. There were colorful, crisp tens and twenties to go into those offering envelopes. And consequently, on Thanksgiving Sunday, each of us clutched our envelope a little more tightly until it landed safely in the offering basket at church.

There was something else different about Thanksgiving Sunday. On that Sunday, all of our offering money went to missions. There was always a spot on the envelope to designate where we wanted our gift to go, and on Thanksgiving Sunday we were all told to mark our envelope for missions. This was Dad's way of saying that we had more than enough. This Sunday was for those who were not so blessed. It was for those people in foreign lands who did not even know about the great God who filled our granaries and loaded down our table with a feast fit for kings.

I am not sure that Dad knew he was bringing Psalm 67 to life, but he was actually doing this psalm. He was making this psalm come alive in front of his family. From the overflow of God's blessing on his life and his family, he was channeling a portion of that blessing to the less fortunate. He was doing this because he wanted the ways of God to be known all over the earth. He wanted the salvation of the LORD to be experienced not just here in Canada, but among all nations.

This is, in fact, a psalm that addresses the nations. It extends beyond the individual or the family. It addresses every ethnic group on the face of the planet with these words: *"May the peoples praise you, O God; may all the peoples praise you. May the nations be glad and sing for joy, for you rule the peoples justly and guide the nations of the earth."*

The God of the universe is calling the peoples of the world to a festival of praise. Through the words of this psalm we are petitioning the LORD over all nations, that His praise would ring forth from all the peoples of the earth. What a glorious day that will be when the nations break forth in joyous songs of praise to their Maker! All of nature testifies to His manifold wisdom. Already, the whole earth is full of His glory. Now our prayer is that all who live on the face of the earth would see that glory and unite in singing His praise. Now that will be a day of thanksgiving—a day like none other!

This call for universal praise is unusual. It is unusual because it draws all of humanity into a common faith. The Jewish faith was and is a very exclusive religion. This is the faith of the chosen people—God's chosen people. They did not choose Him, but rather they were uniquely selected by God to bear His name before the nations of the world. Throughout the Old Testament there is a clear sense that God was dealing with His own special people, and they were to walk separately from the nations. They received God's laws and were the guardians of His commands. They were instructed not to intermarry with other nations nor be polluted by them and their idol worship. The worshippers of Yahweh were an exclusive group, a unique people, but they were not evangelical. They kept the message to themselves.

But here in Psalm 67 the constricted, exclusive God of the Old Testament appears to break out of His narrow nationalist cocoon. We see that He is, in reality, a God for all nations, not just for the descendants of Abraham. Here we catch a glimpse of the big picture—the global perspective. All the nations of the earth are to praise him. The longstanding intent of the God of Israel is that every people group should know His ways and experience His salvation. God's great promise to Abraham will be fulfilled: *"All peoples on earth will be blessed through you"* (Genesis 12:3).

Throughout the Old Testament we can see a certain tension between this global view of the God of the universe and the more restricted nationalist view of God. Most often the old covenant prophets were granted the best view of the God of the big picture— the God who rules over all nations. Isaiah was one such prophet. Let's hear his prophetic word for the nations:

> *See, darkness covers the earth and thick darkness*
> *is over the peoples, but the LORD rises upon you*
> *and his glory appears over you. Nations will*

come to your light, and kings to the brightness of your dawn (Isaiah 60:2–3).

It is the resurrected and ascendant Christ who broke through the thick darkness. He broke the power of the chains of death. He is the One whose light has come. Nations have come to His light and people all over the world continue to come. It is Jesus who broke Judaism out of its narrow bounds and brought the faith of Abraham to the nations. The Light of the World has come. He has caused His face to shine upon us, and now the gift of salvation is available through Him.

This is the greatest cause for thanksgiving. As the resurrected and triumphant Christ stood before His disciples, He gave them this command:

All authority in heaven and on earth has been given to me. Therefore go and make disciples of all nations, baptizing them in the name of the Father and of the Son and of the Holy Spirit, and teaching them to obey everything I have commanded you. And surely I am with you always, to the very end of the age (Matthew 28:18–20).

This statement by Jesus is commonly known as the Great Commission. In Psalm 67 we can see an Old Testament version of the Great Commission. It is a commission that is rooted in thanksgiving and praise. I can only wonder if this is the fount from which all evangelism should flow—not from a browbeaten sense of guilt but from a joy-filled heart of thanksgiving. If we have grasped the fullness of God's blessing on us through Christ, then we are delighted to tell of His great love. We joyously spread the message.

May the peoples praise you, O God; may all the peoples praise you. Then the land will yield its harvest, and God, our God, will bless us. God will bless us, and all the ends of the earth will fear him."

There is a great harvest day that is still coming on the earth. It is not a harvest of wheat, but a harvest of souls that will be swept into the Kingdom of God. If this psalm is to be believed, it is a harvest that is propelled and swelled by our praise. According to our praise it will be gathered in. Who will gather in this harvest? The sad-sack sourpusses of the church need not apply. They can keep their tight-fisted hands in their pockets and their woeful complaints to themselves. The people of praise will see the harvest. With thankful hearts they will bring it home.

Now more than ever Jesus' words ring true: *"You may say there are still four months until harvest time. But I tell you look, and you will see that the fields are ripe and ready to harvest"* (John 4:35 CEV).

Yesterday, I received two e-mail messages from overseas. One was from a young missionary couple who had just arrived in Cambodia, and the other from a missionary couple in China. Their messages reminded me that a great international harvest is coming. It is happening even now. I am thankful that we have the LORD's sure promise on this. Let's dig in. It is harvest time, and even as we praise Him, *"God will bless us, and all the ends of the earth will fear him."*

Bringing Life to the Psalms

1. Read Jesus' discourse on the harvest found in John 4:27–42. Consider that this story took place in Samaria. Jesus was already breaking out of the narrow confines of Judaism. While the disciples were getting food, Jesus was having a feast. What spiritual food sustains your faith?

2. What are some of the family traditions you follow at Thanksgiving? How do those traditions reflect God's goodness to you?

3. Take time today to count your blessings. Too often we focus on our problems and shortcomings, while there is always so much for which to be thankful.

4. Consider making giving a significant part of your Thanksgiving celebration. If you have been blessed, why not make it an opportunity to bless others? Remember, thanksgiving is a valid response to the grace of God at any time of the year.

5. The praise-induced fear of God referred to in this psalm stands in sharp contrast to the man-induced terror that lurks behind demon-inspired religion. The LORD is not the author of intimidation or barrel-of-a-gun conversion. To fear God is to stand in awe of Him—in awe of His mercy, His grace, and His sacrificial love. This awe-inspiring fear is the most direct path to true God-pleasing worship. As you take time to thank God, pray that this wonder-filled awe of God will fall upon all nations.

6. Reread Psalm 67. What is God saying to you by His Spirit?

How Lovely is Your Dwelling Place

Of the Sons of Korah

*How lovely is your dwelling place, O Lord
Almighty!
My soul yearns, even faints, for the courts of
the LORD;
my heart and flesh cry out for the living God.
Even the sparrow has found a home,
and the swallow a nest for herself,
where she may have her young—a place near
your altar,
O LORD Almighty, my King and my God.
Blessed are those who dwell in your house;
they are ever praising you. (Selah)*

MAYBE IT IS BECAUSE CANADIAN
Christendom is architecturally challenged, but images of a church do
not spring to mind when I read the opening lines of this psalm.
Perhaps if I lived in Europe, the lovely dwelling place of the LORD

referred to here would instantly prompt me to imagine one of the grand cathedrals such as Chartres, Notre Dame in Paris, or St. Paul's in London.

Nevertheless, I identify with this psalm. There are times when I am in full agreement with the psalmist. I echo his thoughts. *"My soul yearns, even faints, for the courts of the LORD; my heart and flesh cry out for the living God."*

I want to be with God. I want to be close to Him. I want to be lost in wonder and sense His glory all around me. There are times when I have known that closeness and have experienced that wonder. Now I long for a return to that closeness. Like a desert wanderer yearns for water, I yearn for God. *"My heart and flesh cry out for the living God."*

Sometimes I have found that closeness to God in a church. For me it comes most frequently during times of corporate worship. As songs of praise and worship reach a crescendo, I sense the LORD's nearness; His presence is all around me. At such times it is no great stretch to reach out and touch the Lord as He passes by. He is there in the house of God and, for that time, that precise location is His dwelling place.

There are other times in church when it is the spoken word of God that grabs me. I am under arrest. I have been found by God. I could swear the preacher has been reading my heart and has been following me around all week. He is describing my life—my hidden thought patterns. I have this uncanny sense that this has all been a huge setup. I have been set up by God. He has brought me to this place, backed me into a corner, and now the loving LORD Almighty is pouncing upon me. The Lion of Judah has found His prey. And when it is all over, I am so glad He has. His holy Word has penetrated my heart and I am changed. Into my darkness the Light has come. I walk out of that place with new direction and purpose.

I can only say, *"How lovely is your dwelling place, O LORD Almighty!"*

Despite these wonderful experiences within church buildings, it is not the buildings themselves that attract me though, unlike some people in our society, I certainly have no aversion to church buildings. In the same vein, as someone trained in design I believe I can truly appreciate beautiful architecture in churches and other public buildings. Again, it is not the architecture that attracts me. It is the presence of God that I seek.

Yes, and despite all this, when I read the phrase, *"How lovely is your dwelling place, O LORD Almighty!"* my mind instantly flashes to pictures of nature. I see God there, in the dazzling sunset, in the mountain grandeur, in the forest depths, in expansive prairie vistas, in the wind-whipped ocean breakers, by the sunlit babbling stream. God is there. That is His dwelling place. It is just as David declared, *"The earth is the LORD's, and everything in it, the world, and all who live in it"* (Psalm 24:1).

Nature is God's domain. He formed it, planned it, and spoke it into existence. It is His dwelling place. Our attempts to create a dwelling place for Him are feeble at best. After overseeing the construction of one of the seven wonders of the ancient world, King Solomon, that master temple builder of the Old Testament, declared, *"There is not enough room in heaven for you, LORD God. How can you possibly live on earth in this temple I have built?"* (1 Kings 8:27 CEV).

Our God cannot be contained. He is always spilling over the sides, pushing out of our narrow confines, and showing up in unexpected places.

Perhaps this is to what the psalmist was referring here in Psalm 84, when he discovered that nature had invaded the sanctuary of the LORD. *"Even the sparrow has found a home, and the swallow a nest for herself, where she may have her young—a place near your altar."*

The psalmist's response is very enlightening. He did not see the arrival of these birds in the House of God as something strange or offensive. He did not treat this intrusion of nature as an indignity, ritually prohibited in the earthly residence of Deity. His response is, in fact, just the opposite. He is delighted by his discovery of nesting birds near the altar of God.

The psalmist views the birds' presence as an indication of all of creation's desire to be close to the Creator. The birds are exactly where the psalmist wants to be—permanently in God's presence, constantly singing their LORD's praise. They occupy an envied position. *"Blessed are those who dwell in your house; they are ever praising you."*

And we should note that these birds are not just visiting; they are not passing through. They have made God's house their home. This is their nesting place. Here they will raise their family.

How about you? Where are you nesting? Are you nesting in God's presence? Will you raise your family near the altar of God?

I recall an occasion from my childhood when, at the close of a church service, a barn swallow somehow found its way into our country church. I suppose this bird may have come in through an open front door or possibly through the belfry. Children in the congregation were both excited and amused as this swallow careened about the sanctuary in a display of aerial acrobatics. On the other hand, many of the adults were mortified. After all, this bird might soil the carpet. Quite unexpectedly, nature had invaded the sanctuary of the LORD and the people of God were not entirely pleased.

In retrospect and in light of Psalm 84, I believe the LORD may have been as delighted as the young children with the arrival of that swallow. All our formal church-style stuffiness suddenly went right out the window. The outside had come in. Why not enjoy it? Why not swoop and sing God's praises just like that barn swallow? Why not for a moment be as free as a bird?

Oh, and don't worry about the carpet. Real life is like that. Accidents happen. Humanity isn't clean. That's why there is an altar.

The truly remarkable thing is that the LORD God Almighty chose, and continues to choose, to live with us. He did not confine Himself to the heavens. He chose to swoop down from heaven's heights and nest among us. Sometimes He even shows up in these barns that we call churches. On the day of dedication, without warning, God showed up in Solomon's temple as the priests were singing the LORD's praises.

> *Suddenly a cloud filled the temple as the priests were leaving the holy place. The LORD's glory was in that cloud, and the light from it was so bright that the priests could not stay inside to do their work* (2 Chronicles 5:13–14 CEV).

Why does God choose to do this? Why does He come to live among us? Doesn't He know that we will soil His carpet? We will mess up things. Doesn't He know that the lovely dwelling place of the LORD Almighty will only be lovely until the humans show up? Yet in spite of us and our nest-fouling ways, God chooses to dwell among us.

We can see this clearly in this psalm. Just as the LORD puts up with the nest-building birds and their droppings, so the LORD puts up with us. Actually, God goes beyond putting up with us. He welcomes us. Just as the psalmist expresses his delight with the birds, God is delighted that we have come. He is so glad that we have come into His house, His dwelling place. He is not put off or surprised by our mess-ups.

What parent throws out their infant on the first occasion when they soil their diapers? Every parent knows that baby messes come with the baby. Changing diapers quickly becomes a part of the family routine. As a father of two sons, I had ample opportunity to practice my diaper-changing skills. If the need arose at home, most often my wife or I would use a specially designed change table for this job. I would lay the baby on the change table and in a minute or two, everything was fixed up—put to right—on that change table.

Every rightly-built house of God has a change table. Most often it is called an altar. God fixes us up there. That altar can look quite different depending on which church tradition you follow, but the purpose for the altar is always the same. It is the place where we are cleaned up. Sin is washed away.

God is intimate with us there. The outward trappings of righteousness are stripped away. He sees us completely. You see, there is no place for human pride at the altar of God. Our heavenly Father LORD gently lays us down and does His work on us. There is nothing we can hide. Why would we want to? Let's deal with all of it.

"Cleanse me!" should be our only cry.

Have you been altered at the altar? Has God changed you there—really changed you in the hidden places?

But isn't the altar just for babies? Lord, haven't I grown and matured since my first trip to your altar? I would like to think so. I'm not tripped up by the same things anymore. Surely, I don't have to humble myself yet again!

If we have outgrown the altar, then we have outgrown God. And that's preposterous! The LORD God Almighty has not lost any of His awesome power or majesty simply because we have grown older and supposedly wiser. We are still in need of His correction, His discipline, His mercy, and His love. I still need to get onto God's change table on a regular basis. Moral perfection keeps eluding me. The smugger I feel about my self-deluding, superior spirituality complex, the more I prove that I need to be altered on the altar.

I hear God whispering, "Lay down. Lay it all down. I want to change you."

Over the years I have watched far too many Christians outgrow God. They have become mature in their faith, or so they say, and the altar becomes a place for others to go. Their reasoning goes something like this: "It's a fine place for the wayward and the prodigal, but we are beyond that now."

In my mind I can hear them say, "Since I came to Christ, I have grown in my understanding. I am sure it won't be long and the LORD God Almighty will be calling upon me for advice."

Of course no one would dare say that. But the attitude is there. That superior, older-brother attitude comes to dominate. I know it well because I recognize it in myself.

Soon the house of God loses its appeal. Nature calls. "After all, God is present in nature. I can worship him out by the cottage or down by the lake."

And of course that's true. God can and does meet people in all those locations, and ten thousand other places as well. But is there an altar there? Does God's Word wash over you? Remember, that's where real change happens.

Solomon was right. The great God of the heavens was not content to stay there. The heavens could not contain Him. He swooped down and decided to live among us, to nest with mankind. But God did not stop there. No, the LORD went far beyond that. Through the sacrifice of His Son, He brought us into His nest—into His family.

Wherever I go, I am in His house now. You see, I belong to Him. I'm in the family of God. I am nesting in His presence. And right along with the psalmist I can say, "*How lovely is your dwelling place, O LORD Almighty! My soul yearns, even faints, for the courts of the LORD; my heart and flesh cry out for the living God.*"

And if my heart should stray, "Take me back to your altar, LORD. Cleanse me," is my only cry.

Bringing Life to the Psalms

1. The early chapters of 2 Chronicles recount Solomon's construction and dedication of the temple of the LORD in Jerusalem. The temple of the LORD was the center or focal point for all the Jewish worshippers of *Yahweh*. Have you established a focal point for your family's worship of the LORD? You may wish to read more about this great temple in 2 Chronicles 2 – 7.

2. Does architecture play a role in worship? Can church architecture enhance or hinder your worship experience?

3. What role does nature play in your relationship with God? Do your experiences of nature and the natural environment distract you from worship, or draw you into worship?

4. As we mature in our faith, how can we avoid developing a superior older-brother attitude?

From Strength to Strength

Blessed are those whose strength is in you,
who have set their hearts on pilgrimage.
As they pass through the Valley of Baca,
they make it a place of springs;
the autumn rains also cover it with pools.
They go from strength to strength,
till each appears before God in Zion.
Hear my prayer, O LORD God Almighty;
listen to me, O God of Jacob. (Selah)
Look upon our shield, O God;
look with favor on your anointed one.

TO BE PERFECTLY HONEST, I DIS-
graced myself. At least that's how I saw it then, and how I see it now.
I entered a marathon and had to pull out at mile twenty-three. My
friend, Glen, had persuaded me to join him on this venture and, right

from the start, I had very few misgivings. I was confident that I was up to the challenge. After all, I was a young, healthy, college student. I was used to heavy farm work during the summer. Certainly this would be something I could handle—or so I thought.

It all began well enough. It was a beautiful Saturday morning in spring, and thousands of people had turned out to participate in the twenty-six-mile event. Glen and I were excited to be part of the March for Millions, a fundraiser to help the hungry in Third World countries. It seemed like half the population of the city set out from the starting point. It was great!

The first few miles went fine. By mile eight, I was beginning to tire. By mile ten, I had developed a large blister on the sole of my foot. By mile twelve, the blister had broken and was bleeding. Soon other blisters were popping up like whack-a-moles at a county fair midway. The next few miles were pure agony. Every muscle in my legs was screaming for this torture to end.

All the while, Glen stuck with me, encouraging me, urging me on. My friend was doing fine. He was still bouncing around like a young colt out for a morning frolic in spring.

By mile twenty-one my pace had slowed and my gait was uneven. At mile twenty-three I hit the proverbial wall. Participants were dropping out like milk house flies caught in a fog of DDT. This was insanity; I could go no further. Some kind volunteer drove me back to the college while the still-energetic Glen went onto complete the full marathon.

My marathon experience was the complete antithesis of what is described in this portion of Psalm 84. Though I set my heart on this twenty-six-mile pilgrimage, I did not go from strength to strength. Just the opposite happened. My strength was drained away and I never reached my end goal, the finish line, my personal Zion.

In retrospect, it is not difficult to determine why I failed while my friend succeeded. While he was active on the basketball team through the winter season, I was lounging around the dorm. While he daily walked a mile to the college, I walked a few steps from the dorm to the academic center. While he was trying out for the track team, I was checking out the cheerleaders. My summertime muscle had turned marshmallow soft by the time spring rolled around. Glen was ready for the challenge; I was ready for the couch.

How about you? Are you ready for life's great pilgrimage? Have you set your sights on Zion? Will you succeed in your faith walk or will you fall short of the great goal? Will you disgrace yourself as I did?

The pilgrimage experience is something with which most twenty-first-century believers are unfamiliar. But pilgrimage was a common, community-wide experience for all residents of biblical Israel. It was decreed by Moses in the Book of the Law:

> *Three times a year all your men must appear before the LORD your God at the place he will choose: at the Feast of Unleavened Bread, the Feast of Weeks and the Feast of Tabernacles. No man should appear before the LORD empty-handed. Each of you must bring a gift in proportion to the way the LORD your God has blessed you* (Deuteronomy 16:16–17).

In actual practice for the devout of Israel, this became a regular, routine event—a family pilgrimage to the temple in Jerusalem. The whole clan would pack up and travel in large caravans to the holy city. Much of biblical literature and history is centered on these pilgrimages. In fact, many of the psalms were written for the community to sing or chant as they made their way to Jerusalem. The Songs of Ascents— Psalm 120 through to Psalm 134—were specifically written for this purpose. With this in mind, here in Psalm 84 we read, "*Blessed are those whose strength is in you, who have set their hearts on pilgrimage.*"

To the Jewish faithful of biblical times, these words would bring memories of many miles travelled on dusty roads to Jerusalem. For many pilgrims, this was a long and arduously painful journey made on foot. From Galilee to Jerusalem is almost seventy miles (one-hundred-thirteen kilometers). This trip was no quick one-day trot. It was a multi-day journey, challenging even for the physically fit. Weary bones, aching muscles, and blistered feet were undoubtedly a common occurrence. Strength was needed for the journey.

Where did that strength come from? For many, there was strength and encouragement from family and friends. People walked and talked together. They visited, swapped stories, reconnected with their sons and daughters, and renewed lapsed friendships. The miles go by quicker in the company of faithful friends.

We catch a glimpse of all this in Luke's account of Jesus' boyhood Passover pilgrimage to Jerusalem. On the return trip we are told that Mary and Joseph thought Jesus was *"traveling with some other people, and they went a whole day before they started looking for him. When they could not find him with their relatives and friends, they went back to Jerusalem and started looking for him there"* (Luke 2:44–45 CEV).

With our post-modern fear of strangers harming our children, we may see in this story an example of parental irresponsibility. In reality, it illustrates the strong sense of both family and community that existed among these pilgrims. They looked after one another, and together they journeyed in fellowship as one body. They were knit together by the bonds of faith, family, and friendship. The common experience of this annual pilgrimage cemented their love and commitment to one another. The nuclear family was so fused to the broader family of faith that it created a strong sense of mutual trust and responsibility.

We are called to a faith journey despite our collective ignorance about pilgrimage during biblical times. After our initial introduction to Christ, we all find ourselves on a sacred pilgrimage. Many set out on this journey to the eternal arms of Christ, but there are many who fall by the wayside, unable or unwilling to continue the walk of faith. What characteristics mark the winners from the losers in this great marathon of faith? How can we ensure that we will make it safely to the other side of the finish line?

We have already discovered one way to ensure success in our pilgrimage of faith. We are to undertake this walk together. This is a community walk. It is to be undertaken with family and friends at our side. Even in my failed marathon attempt, I had a faithful friend by my side. On my own, I likely would have quit at mile fifteen, but with Glen's encouragement I persisted for another eight miles. Pity the man or woman who has no fellowship on the journey—no one to boost their faith or urge them on.

The fellowship and regular encouragement of believers is essential if we are to succeed in this lifelong marathon of faith. Join yourself to a church—a family of faith—that is journeying together with you to Zion, to the arms of Christ. Though your walk is yours alone, every marathoner needs a support team. If you are sincere about reaching Zion, you will welcome all the help you can get. This is not a trip for the self-isolating loner.

I cannot think of marathons without being reminded of Terry Fox. This incredible one-legged runner made it halfway across Canada in his great one-man pilgrimage to raise funds for cancer research. He ran the equivalent of a marathon a day for four and a half months from April 12 to September 1, 1980. Most marathoners require a week or more to repair muscle and recharge their energy supply after the grueling exertion of the run, but Terry was back on the road the next day to do it all over again. The stamina required defies description. Accomplishing such a feat on two legs is incredible; doing it on one leg and a severed stump quite simply boggles the mind.

Only a super-elite athlete could hope to achieve what Terry Fox did. Physical conditioning is essential for success, but what about spiritual conditioning? If we are going to accomplish awesome things in God's Kingdom, there is a spiritual conditioning that needs to take place inside of us. After all, Christ, the Captain of our faith, has called us to be disciples, not bench-warmers.

Pilgrimage is not a spectator sport, but many view their Christian faith that way. The reasoning goes something like this: It's fine for the paid clergy to engage in faith exercises such as regular Bible reading, fasting, and prayer. Isn't that why we pay them? The rest of us are busy with life's daily grind.

The busy, world-engaged laity is far too often content to coast on the second-hand faith of church leadership. In reality, our own faith muscles need development and regular exercise. If regular spiritual conditioning isn't taking place, we become weak in our faith. We are fit for the couch, not the pilgrim's route. We stumble when others question our beliefs. Temptations overwhelm us. Doubts drain us of our spiritual vitality. We conform to the thinking of this world. We are not reaching the world with the message of Christ; the world is reaching us, and pressing us into its mold.

But there is a different path for us to walk, an upward path. Christ has gone ahead and He has prepared that path for us. Following that path will lead us to the grandest adventure imaginable. We have the assurance of His presence, His encouragement, and His help for the journey. His blessing goes with us, and here in Psalm 84 we have the sure promise of His unfailing Word: *"Blessed are those whose strength is in you, who have set their hearts on pilgrimage."*

Our strength truly is in Him. He is our forerunner who has cleared the way. In fact, He is the *way*. On His last earthly Passover pilgrimage, Jesus walked the way of the cross, and it is the way of the cross that will bring us safely into His arms. There is no greater pilgrimage—no other route we can take to Zion, our eternal home.

Our strength is not in prayer. It is not in fasting. It is not in the discipline of daily Bible reading or Bible study. All of these spiritual disciplines have value. They are exercises that enhance our level of spiritual conditioning. They turn our marshmallow flab into rock-hard spiritual muscle. But our strength does not come from them. Our strength is in the LORD. Strength for our pilgrimage comes only from Him.

We can pray from dusk to dawn, but unless the Son of Righteousness shines upon us, we are calling out in vain. We can fast for forty days, but unless the Bread of Life meets with us and sustains us, our sacrifice has no value. We can read God's Holy Word daily, but unless Jesus walks off those pages and into our lives, the exercise is meaningless.

Christ is our strength for the journey. We undertake these disciplines in order to meet with Him, in order to hear His voice, in order to see His will and His purposes accomplished. Spiritual disciplines are a means to reach our source. But prayer is not our source—Jesus is. It is essential that we hear from Him when we pray, meet with Him as we fast, discover His will for us as we meditate on His Word. Then we will have strength for the journey because He will be the strength within us. He will be the *way* beneath our feet. He will be to us the Bread of Life that nourishes and sustains us on the pilgrimage. He will be the Living Water for our thirsty soul.

Only with Christ in us can we turn the Valley of Baca into a place of springs. *Baca* is the Hebrew word for weeping. The place of weeping becomes a place of living springs when Jesus passes by. Christ in us can make that happen. He is the great transformer, bringing light into darkness, joy into hearts of sorrow, hope into the Valley of Despair.

You see, our pilgrimage is not just for our benefit. We are on this journey to bring pleasure to the heart of our heavenly Father, and his Spirit prompts us to bring Christ's love to all the travelers we meet on this road of life. In our own strength this is an impossible task, a daily uphill marathon without an end in sight. But if we meet daily with the One who is our strength, this is a doable task—no, an enjoyable privilege.

Best of all, we will be numbered among the throng that crosses the finish line. Then it will be said of us, *"They go from strength to strength, till each appears before God in Zion."*

Bringing Life to the Psalms

1. Over a two-week period, consider doing a daily reading through "The Songs of Ascents," Psalm 120 through to Psalm 134. What insights are you able to glean from these psalms? Can you see how the theme of pilgrimage is integral to these psalms?

2. Have you ever undertaken a major endeavor and fallen short of your goal? What did you learn from that experience? Sometimes we learn far more from our failures than from our successes. How have your failures helped to shape your life? Remember that God can turn our failures into stepping stones to success.

3. Are you building spiritual muscle or turning into a faithless couch potato? What spiritual disciplines are you exercising on a regular basis? Choose a spiritual discipline to focus on this week. Set an achievable goal, such as ten minutes of daily prayer. If you are in a study group, report back to others on your ability to meet that goal.

4. What can church leadership do to increase the sense of group pilgrimage within your congregation? Can you think of ways to build a greater sense of connectedness within your faith community? What role might God want you to play in this regard?

The Best Day

Better is one day in your courts than a
thousand elsewhere;
I would rather be a doorkeeper in the house of
my God
than dwell in the tents of the wicked.
For the LORD God is a sun and a shield;
the LORD bestows favor and honor;
no good thing does he withhold
from those whose walk is blameless.
O LORD Almighty, blessed is the man
who trusts in you.

YESTERDAY WAS MY WIFE'S
birthday. What a day it was! After a quick read through my morning devotions and a hasty breakfast, I rushed off to my teaching job on the other side of the city. The teaching day was particularly

129

demanding. Not all teenagers are intellectual sponges, eager to soak up wisdom from the fount of learning. Instead, many minds are locked behind cold steel doors. Reaching them is a challenge; teaching them is nigh impossible unless you find the unique key for their particular mental doors. And sometimes students change the locks in the middle of the night, so what worked yesterday will not work today. That's all part of the challenge of teaching young teens.

After a full day of doing mental acrobatics and verbal jousting before 120 young minds, it was time to sit down and write report card comments for the parents of those same children. For two and a half hours, I made a substantive start on this onerous task. At last, in the mid-November dark, I got into my car for the long commute home. Heavy rain, a stalled car in my lane, and bumper-to-bumper freeway traffic reduced my progress to a crawl.

I had a stop to make before reaching home—the flower store. As I stood inside the flower cooler, a dozen autumn-yellow roses caught my eye. They put a spark into my wife's eyes as well when I presented them just before dinner. Actually, my wife and son had already started dinner. They had given up waiting for me. Fortunately, the oven-baked frozen pizza was still warm. It tasted good, mostly because I was hungry at the end of a long day.

In the rush of life, some days are better than others. A special day like a birthday is meant to be a better day, a special day above the norm. It should be marked by moments of warmth and friendship. But too often that's all there is—a brief moment. The day plunges forward with demanding routines that rob us of intimacy. Instead of something special, we are left with all the relational warmth of a cold, dry pizza crust.

On a personal note, I think my wife's birthday should be declared a national holiday! Then, as a family, we could celebrate the day together in a manner more in keeping with her worth and her importance to the well-being of us all. But alas, the chances of this happening are remote indeed. Though I believe she is worthy of the honor, I am not sure the prime minister and his cabinet could be persuaded to my point of view.

Levity aside, we do need special days. They are essential to the maintenance of any healthy relationship. Despite my stress-filled day, my wife's birthday actually did go largely according to plan. Because of my hectic schedule, we decided in advance to hold off on our celebrations until the weekend. On Saturday, at a more leisurely pace, we went out to her favorite restaurant. We followed up with a trip to see a friend who is a custom jewelry designer. I bought her a rare agate pin that will always remind her of our love, of good times spent with friends and family, and a special day in her honor that we spent together.

Really, all of Psalm 84 is written in praise of a special day—a day spent in God's presence. Throughout this psalm there is a longing to be with God, a desire to be close to Him. We hear the psalmist declare, *"Better is one day in your courts than a thousand elsewhere."*

If you were to plan for the best day in your life, what would that day include? What would it look like? How and where would you spend your best day? Would the LORD be at the center of it all?

Love is at the core of every special day. Think back to some of the best days of your life—days marked by joy and excitement. If you scratch beneath the surface of those days, you will find love at the core.

We are in fact love-starved people. We need love as much as the air we breathe. Experiments have shown that the unloved, uncaressed, unspoken-to baby will die even though all its physical needs are met. So when love comes to us, we celebrate it, frolic in it, and throw a party to announce it.

Some of the best days of my life were falling-in-love days. To think someone loved me, simply wanted to be with me—well, it put a real bounce in my step. To be more accurate, it fried all my circuits. Thinking of her made me dreadfully forgetful. I would routinely forget what I was doing mid-task. I was noted for being calm and sedate. Now, suddenly, I was doing outrageous, crazy things. Love has a special way of breaking down barriers and freeing us from inhibitions. Real love is never rational; it doesn't make sense.

We need love. We need to receive it. We need to give it.

It was love that brought the psalmist to the House of God. It drew him like a magnet, pulled at his heart, tugged at his sleeve, and finally ushered him through the door. Love set him on this pilgrimage. It kept his weary feet moving, mile after dreary mile. When he finally reached his goal—the object of his love—we hear him exclaim in wonder, "*How lovely is your dwelling place, O LORD Almighty! My soul yearns, even faints, for the courts of the LORD; my heart and flesh cry out for the living God.*"

In reality, Psalm 84 is a love poem. It is all about the psalmist's quest for love. These opening lines express it best. The psalmist is thirsting for a drink from heaven's Eternal Fount of Love. He yearns, faints, and cries out for the living God. He expresses all this in what any poet would call the language of love. Here we see the psalmist as the love-starved lover in search of the Divine Love of his soul.

This hunger and thirst for love is, in fact, a recurring theme throughout the Psalms and, indeed, all of Holy Scripture. Psalm 42 begins with these words: "*As the deer pants for streams of water, so my soul pants for you, O God. My soul thirsts for God, for the living God. When can I go and meet with God?*" (Psalm 42:1–2).

Best days are days spent in pursuit of love, with the one we love. We yearn for such times. This pursuit of love is what drives the sales of a thousand romance novel titles. It is the wellspring for a million songs. It powers a large part of the movie industry. It turns Valentine's Day into a global celebration.

The psalmist was pursuing love with the One he loved—the LORD Almighty. Have you spent time pursuing Him lately? Is a day spent with Him something you yearn for? Or are you embarrassed by the blatant language of love that the psalmist uses here? Do hymns of praise and worship choruses bore you?

All true worship is an act of love. It extols the virtues of the One we love, and it delights in simply being together. It unites the worshipped with the worshipper.

"Better is one day in your courts than a thousand elsewhere; I would rather be a doorkeeper in the house of my God than dwell in the tents of the wicked."

There is no better place to be than with the one you love. If I know the love of God, I can bask in that love, relax in it, and dance to it. Why would I want to be anywhere else? I am satisfied in His arms of love—arms that reach out to me. There is no temptation for the fully satisfied. The tents of the wicked hold no allure.

The best place is the place of the greatest love, and when the LORD Almighty is our lover, we can rest assured that there is no shortage of love. He did not spare His Son in His pursuit of love, but rather offered Him up for us. He let nothing come between us, not even our filthy load of sin. By the death of His Son, He removed it. Forever! Oh, what a Lover!

Why would I want to be with Him? The answer is obvious: I am safe and affirmed with the One I love. He treats me well. *"For the LORD God is a sun and a shield; the LORD bestows favor and honor."*

The LORD God brightens my day. He puts a spring in my step and a glint in my eye. Love has a way of doing that.

The LORD God surrounds and covers me with His shield. I am protected by Him. He is my pillar of fire by night. No marauder can invade this hallowed sanctum and steal me away. After all, *"I am my beloved's and my beloved is mine ... and his banner over me was love"* (Song of Solomon 6:3, 2:4 NKJV).

"The LORD bestows favor and honor." A lover will do that, and this Divine Lover certainly does. He showers me with blessings. There are countless blessings, and they are so undeserved and some-

times they are so unexpected. So often He takes me completely by surprise. Lovers do that sort of thing. I know He must delight in seeing the look of surprise on my face as He blesses me in some new, phenomenal way.

The LORD's love is extravagant. How extravagant, you ask? Well, we have this promise—this assertion—here in this psalm: *"No good thing does he withhold from those whose walk is blameless."*

There is a huge extravagance in that assertion. I can think of plenty of things that are good: friendship, health, prosperity, and fruitful days, to name just a few. This Lover of my soul withholds none of these from me. His hand of blessing is always held open wide to me. The good God I serve does only good things, and in this respect He has proven Himself to me over and over again. I can trust Him. Only one condition applies, and that is that my walk be blameless.

May my prayer ever be for a blameless walk, for a life lived in pleasing Him.

It is the extravagance of God's love that should motivate each of us to live a blameless life. The apostle Paul reminds us of this when he states, *"He who did not spare his own Son, but gave him up for us all—how will he not also, along with him, graciously give us all things?"* (Romans 8:32).

There He goes again—promising me the world. Lovers are a bit crazy that way, quite irrational. In the above passage, God is promising with Christ to *"graciously give us all things."*

Now, that's a bit rich. Except this Lover of mine really is rich—rich beyond measure. Bill Gates is a lowly pauper before Him. If my Lover promises the world, He can deliver. And He will deliver. The One who formed the world will turn it over to us—to my Lover and me. That's His promise.

You see, the day will come when I am going to reign with Him. I have His word on it. Actually, I am reigning in life right now, through Him. Again His Word assures me that *"those who receive*

God's abundant provision of grace and the gift of righteousness reign in life through the one man, Jesus Christ" (Romans 5:17).

But the big day—the best day—is still coming: the day of consummation. The wedding feast of the Lamb will be the best day of all. No other day can match it. We will see Him face to face. I don't know about you, but I have had enough of this long distance loving.

Some day soon, He is coming.

Some day soon, I'm going with Him. Some day soon …

The bride of Christ, perfected through suffering, will be caught up to meet Him in the air. This Lover will literally sweep us off our feet. He will sweep us off our feet and take us home to His house. Some day soon …

The best day? It's still coming. It is coming soon.

As in eager anticipation I await that day—the best day—may these words be my constant testimony: "O LORD Almighty, blessed is the man who trusts in you!"

Bringing Life to the Psalms

1. If you were to plan for the best day in your life, what would that day include? Why not plan to spend a day—a special day—with the LORD? This may involve getting away to a retreat centre where you can focus on the Lover of your soul. Consider what things you might do together to make this a special day—the best day—spent with Him.

2. Is there a hymn or worship chorus you love, that ushers you into God's throne room? Sing it to Him. Sing it over and over. Let it be your love song for the day or for however long it resonates between you and the One you love.

3. A sense of place can be important. Is there a physical place where you feel closer to God? It could be at church, at home, or somewhere out in nature. Spend some intimate moments there. We can't always make the grand pilgrimage, but lovers find time—they make time—to be together.

4. The psalmist exclaims, "O LORD Almighty, *blessed is the man who trusts in you!*" Do you find your trust in God growing day by day? Trust is relaxed, never agitated. It grows best in a sunny place. Plan some Son time this week.

5. Reread all of Psalm 84. What is God saying to you by His Spirit?

Praise the LORD, O my Soul

Of David

Praise the Lord , O my soul;
all my inmost being, praise his holy name.
Praise the LORD, O my soul, and forget not all
his benefits —
who forgives all your sins and heals all your
diseases,
who redeems your life from the pit and crowns
you with love and compassion,
who satisfies your desires with good things
so that your youth is renewed like the eagle's.

THE LONG WAIT WAS FINALLY over. It was a beautiful day, and it all started so well. Anticipation does make the heart grow fonder. For many years, my wife had told me how she wanted her own desk and her own bookcase. It would help her organize her things; every woman needs her own space. I couldn't agree more. The only problem was money—there was never enough of it. With a young family and a mortgage to pay, there always seemed to be more month left than money. These extras were always put on hold.

Then one spring day our income tax refund check arrived and Karen renewed her perennial plea. This year the roof didn't need shingles, the driveway didn't need paving, but she did need that long-delayed desk and bookcase. At long last, the time had come to answer her request and this time a shortage of funds was not standing in the way.

After some judicious shopping, she narrowed the range of furniture choices, then brought me in to help in the final selection process. Together we chose a compact and versatile three-drawer desk with a fold-down top that acted as the writing surface. She loved the little compartments that could be used to store papers and valuables. A matching three-shelf bookcase completed our order. Both selections were unfinished furniture made of solid maple.

We both love solid wood because of its grain and texture. Of course, solid hardwood furniture is supremely durable as well. I gave some consideration to finishing the furniture myself. But a look at my work schedule led us to decide it would be easier to have the furniture company apply the wood finish of our choice, and then we would pick up the finished product upon completion. We paid our hard-earned money and waited.

About a week later the call came. The desk and bookcase were ready for pick up. But our car was too small for the job. No problem. Our neighbor kindly lent us his pickup truck. Now this old Ford had seen better days. Rick briefly introduced me to old Betsy. He mentioned the rear tailgate was a bit cantankerous. I practiced closing it. Then he handed me the keys and watched as I drove off with my wife by my side. We headed off like two giddy kids on a Christmas morning race to the tree.

At the furniture warehouse, the bookcase and desk were packed in corrugated cardboard boxes. We did a quick inspection to confirm they were the right pieces finished with the right stain and then we loaded them onto old Betsy. I slammed the tailgate shut and we set out on the twenty-minute return trip to our home.

What happened on that return trip can best be described as tragic comedy. However, it would be fair to say that the comedic elements in this story were not entirely evident to us at the time.

On the four-lane expressway at 100 kilometers per hour (60 miles an hour), old Betsy's tailgate popped open. The bookcase toppled out onto the hard black asphalt. I slammed on the brakes and pulled off to the shoulder. My wife was frantic; we were both frantic. Even at a distance I could tell the bookcase was probably still intact inside the corrugated cardboard box. Perhaps the damage was minor, or so I hoped. I jumped out of the truck and began running back to this hapless box as it lay on the highway. Three quarters of it lay on the paved shoulder—only one corner protruded onto the far right lane of the busy four-lane expressway. As I ran back, several cars zoomed right by it. They didn't even need to swerve to avoid it.

I thought it was safe.

But ...

But ... the next vehicle was a twenty-ton cement truck. It did not swerve. It bore down relentlessly on that cardboard box. What I saw next was an explosion. On impact, the bookcase exploded out of its cardboard box. Shelves and splintered pieces of wood went flying through the air and into the ditch.

It all happened so fast. In an instant our long-awaited treasure was turned into a mangled, splintered mess.

I gathered the debris out of the ditch, put it back in old Betsy, slammed the cantankerous tailgate shut, and drove on home.

Karen was in tears.

This should never have happened! A thousand regrets flooded my mind. Why? Why this disaster? What did we do to deserve this mess?

I hugged my wife.

Strangely, on another level, a different set of thoughts was welling up from within. They went something like this: *"In everything give thanks: for this is the will of God in Christ Jesus for you"* (1 Thessalonians 5:18 NKJV).

And then from the distant recesses of my spirit I heard, *"Praise the LORD, O my soul; all my inmost being, praise his holy name. Praise the LORD, O my soul, and forget not all his benefits"* (Psalm 103:1–2).

What lunacy is this? Why should I give thanks to God in the middle of this disaster? If God cared about me—about us—why didn't He prevent this fiasco? My God is bigger than a cement truck. He could have steered that twenty-ton behemoth around our bookcase. Better still, the LORD Almighty could have kept that tailgate from popping open. And now, at this moment, I'm supposed to praise Him? What insanity is this?

Again I heard the Spirit's prompting, *"Praise the LORD, O my soul; all my inmost being, praise his holy name. Praise the LORD, O my soul, and forget not all his benefits."*

There are bigger things in life than a broken bookcase, I conceded. Under my breath I began to mumble, *"Bless the LORD, O my soul and all that is within me, bless his holy name."*

Those were tough words to say at that moment. You see, my soul doesn't always want to bless the LORD. If I'm going to praise Him, shouldn't it be in church while the choir sings softly in the background? Why praise Him on an expressway, with my wife sobbing at my side, and while I have fresh images of a splintered bookcase lodged in my brain?

There are times when cursing the LORD would seem to be a far more appropriate response than praising Him. Surely this was one such time.

"Be joyful always; pray continually; give thanks in all circumstances, for this is God's will for you in Christ Jesus" (1 Thessalonians 5:16–18).

"LORD, why are You bringing these Scriptures to my mind now?" I asked. "I would much rather blame You, God, and feel totally miserable, than give thanks in these wretched circumstances."

But God's Spirit would not relent. I can't say I heard this audibly. But if I were to translate what I felt God was saying to me at that moment, it would go something like this:

"Just shut up. Quit your bellyaching, Mr. Know-it-all." (God sometimes needs to be blunt with me.) "All I am asking you to do is praise Me. Praise Me, whether you feel like it or not. You don't know the beginning from the end, Mr. Wise-guy. Don't you think I'm bigger than a few pieces of shattered wood?"

In sullen reluctance, I agreed. I obeyed. I began to praise God. That's right. I began to praise the LORD God Almighty who let my wife's long-awaited, brand new, not-even-out-of-the-box bookcase get hit by a twenty-ton cement truck.

Praise the LORD? Yes, the LORD.

Now which LORD was that again?

The LORD *"who forgives all your sins and heals all your diseases."*

Ah, yes, that LORD. He really is quite wonderful. Imagine forgiving *all* my sins, every last one of them. That's a lot of sins.

That's a lot of forgiving.

Praise the LORD. He's quite some God.

Which God was that again?

The LORD who *"heals all your diseases."*

Ah yes, that LORD. He really is quite fantastic. Imagine healing *all* my sicknesses, and *all* my injuries too from my childhood to this very moment. Now that's a whole lot of pain and woe.

Gone. It's all gone. I don't feel any of it now.

Praise the LORD. No aches or pains—that's amazing. He's an awesome God.

Now tell me again, which LORD is this?

The LORD *"who redeems your life from the pit and crowns you with love and compassion."*

Oh yes, that LORD. He redeemed me—redeemed me with His blood. He went to the whipping post, was stripped naked, and nailed through hands and feet to a cross. The LORD who was despised and rejected. The LORD who came to His own, but His own would not receive him. That forsaken LORD who loved me to death. The LORD my Redeemer, that's the LORD I praise.

I praise the One who pulled me out of the pit—the pit of self-pity, the pit of despair, the sucking pit of self-indulgence that spirals only downwards. He redeemed me from that sinking pit. And now He is the One I praise.

But He doesn't just redeem. He crowns me with love and compassion. Now that is beyond amazing. Though I do not deserve it, He puts a crown of love on my head. He wore a crown of thorns, but on my head He puts a crown of love and compassion. He encircles my head—my stubborn, sin-drenched head—with love and compassion. Awesome. What an awesome God!

Praise the LORD!

I'm a bit slow today, God. Remember I've got a splintered bookcase on my brain. Could You just remind me—remind me one more time? Which LORD are You?

The LORD *"who satisfies your desires with good things, so that your youth is renewed like the eagle's."*

Oh yes, LORD, You do satisfy me. You satisfy me with a thousand good things. I live like a king. My every need is met; every comfort is mine. I have abundance. Compared to billions on this planet today, and compared to billions going back through the ages, I am blessed— blessed beyond measure.

You renew my strength. You put a glint in my eye, a spring in my step, and a well of hope in my heart. My youth is renewed like the eagle's. Now I'm soaring. Praise the LORD!

I said, "Praise the LORD! Praise the LORD, O my soul!"

I was feeling much better by the time I got home, and so was my wife.

As for that bookcase, I'm glancing at it even as I write this chapter. It looks great! Some carpentry clamps and a little wood glue can work wonders. Despite being hit by a twenty-ton cement truck, only one shelf was broken beyond repair. While I was replacing that shelf at a wood shop in a school nearby, I was encouraged by a friend to take a university course in design and technology. That course rerouted my whole teaching career. It brought me into a line of work I simply love. I started on that new route because of a broken bookcase. Praise the LORD!

I said, "Praise the LORD, O my soul!"

Yes, praise the LORD! In any situation, it is one of the best things this cantankerous soul can do.

Bringing Life to the Psalms

1. The well-known adage, "prayer changes things," should be joined by its lesser-known cousin, "praise changes things." How do you think an attitude of praise worked to change things in the real-life account you just read? How is a praise response possible during difficult circumstances?

2. What are the first words to come out of your mouth when something bad happens? If we change our reaction, can we affect the longer-term outcomes from a negative event?

3. Praise changes our point of view. We look up at God instead of our circumstances. His perspective on the events in our life is completely different from our own. He does see the beginning from the

end. He has the full picture. Genuine praise and worship elevates us. By the Spirit, it brings us above our situation. Remember things always look different when viewed from above.

4. Reread Psalm 103 or, better yet, memorize it. Begin to build a foundation of praise in your life. It will help you weather many a storm.

5. To start your day tomorrow, read Psalm 100. Let your praise to God flow like a river.

Our God, the Extremist

*The LORD works righteousness and justice for all the
oppressed.
He made known his ways to Moses, his deeds to
the people of Israel:
The LORD is compassionate and gracious, slow to
anger, abounding in love.
He will not always accuse, nor will he harbor his
anger forever;
he does not treat us as our sins deserve
or repay us according to our iniquities.
For as high as the heavens are above the earth,
so great is his love for those who fear him;
as far as the east is from the west,
so far has he removed our transgressions from us.
As a father has compassion on his children,
so the LORD has compassion on those who fear him;
for he knows how we are formed, he remembers
that we are dust.
As for man, his days are like grass, he flourishes
like a flower of the field;
the wind blows over it and it is gone, and its place
remembers it no more.*

But from everlasting to everlasting the LORD's love is
with those who fear him,
and his righteousness with their children's children —
with those who keep his covenant and remember to
obey his precepts.

IT IS WELL WORTH NOTING THAT
David wrote Psalm 103. David was a man of extremes; he lived life to
the full. Never one to rest on his laurels, he was always up for a challenge and if no challenge existed, he would create one for himself. He
was a man's kind of man, not easily discouraged or deterred, ready to
throw himself headlong into the fray. Undoubtedly, others saw and
admired these qualities in him. That's why they gathered around him
and stuck with him through the extremes, the highs and lows of a life
lived fully and unreservedly for God.

Sometimes I wonder what David would be like if we met him
today, if he lived in today's world. Into what endeavor would he throw
his boundless energy? Who are the extreme men, the Davids of our
time? Who are the men—or the women, for that matter—who take
on the Goliaths of our present world?

This gutsy determination was evident throughout David's long
and eventful life. As a young teenager, a mere scamp, David had the
in-your-face audacity to take on Goliath, the towering, undefeated
Philistine champion. The battle was no game of tiddlywinks, no
computer simulation. This was mortal combat—the real thing, winner take all—including your severed head (1 Samuel 17).

Do we have any young Davids—any teens—who with God on
their side, will step out from the crowd and risk all in the defense of
faith and truth?

Later as a young man, we find David at Ziklag. After a meteoric
start to his career, he has plummeted from favor. He has persevered
through round after round of downward spiraling misfortune. Now

at his lowest point, with his own men about to stone him, he rises above an embittered throng of naysayers and doubters. With his very life in the balance, he finds strength in the LORD his God. Then, by the extraordinary grace of his God, this indefatigable David pursues his enemies. He seizes victory by the sandal straps and refuses—absolutely refuses—to let it escape over the next hill (1 Samuel 30).

Do we have any never-give-up, never-say-die Davids like that today? Or do we give up at the first sign of opposition? It takes young men of extreme faith to persevere in the face of an unrelenting foe. Have you seen a David lately?

A middle-aged David faced betrayal and heartbreak as his own son, Absalom, sought to kill him and wrench the kingdom from his faltering hands. As this grand tragedy unfolds, David humbles himself before God and his people. He flees Jerusalem barefoot, weeping, and with his head covered as a sign of deep contrition (2 Samuel 15:30). The God of all mercy hears his prayers and restores the fallen king—the repentant king—to the throne. Sometimes humility takes far more courage than a strutting, cocksure leader can muster. But King David—the man at the top—still knew how to humble himself. He knew how to repent.

What a stark contrast to the middle-aged barons of business and banking who in recent years have been hauled before the courts in disgrace. All we hear from them is denial, denial, and lie follows lie. Men are a strange lot. Once the great ego puffs itself up, it seems to be incapable of self-deflation. We cannot prick our own balloons.

Do we have any top-of-their-game Davids who know how to humble themselves before God and before the public, and openly repent? Upper echelon Davids like that are in extremely short supply, perhaps even extinct. Have you caught a glimpse of one?

In his old age David looked ahead. With a prophet's eye he saw the future and he planned for a nation without him. He installed his son Solomon on the throne, but he placed the LORD at the helm of Israel, even as the LORD had always been at the helm of David's entire life. Now in his last days, the House of God became David's prime concern. He was not permitted to build the temple of the LORD (1 Chronicles 17), but he made extensive preparations for it. Upon David's death, the House of God would rise. How like another descendant of David—upon Jesus' death, by the power of the Spirit, the Church of God would arise.

In his instructions to his son Solomon, David says,

> *"I have taken great pains to provide for the temple of the LORD a hundred thousand talents of gold, a million talents of silver, quantities of bronze and iron too great to be weighed, and wood and stone"* (1 Chronicles 22:14).

Do we have any end-of-life Davids like that today? Will you leave behind a visible legacy to the LORD's great goodness? What preparations are you making that will honor God for generations yet to come? Remember: a life lived for God never ends and its influence never ceases.

Consider this: David is still influencing lives today—far more lives, in fact, than he did three thousand years ago. Though Solomon's temple no longer stands, David's words—his psalms of praise to God—resound in every nation under heaven. Now that's a legacy of faith—extreme faith!

The world needs far more faithful-to-the-LORD Davids. We need them at every stage of life. If biblical Davids like that are in short supply in today's world, why not decide to become one yourself? Never underestimate what God can do through a life that is wholly yielded to Him. When complacency is replaced by extreme, in-touch-with-God faith, anything is possible.

Let's look verse-by-verse at what David wrote in Psalm 103 about the wonderful God he served throughout his life. David declares, "*The* LORD *works righteousness and justice for all the oppressed.*"

When David was oppressed by Saul, he did not give up, nor did he take vengeance into his own hands. He entrusted his ultimate fate to the LORD. And the LORD saw; He took note of His servant David. Saul falsely accused David of rebellion, but David was a faithful servant both to King Saul and to the LORD, the highest king. David waited on God and, ultimately, he saw the LORD work righteousness and justice on his behalf. Saul was defeated by the Philistines and, in due course, faithful David ascended to the throne.

"*He made known his ways to Moses, his deeds to the people of Israel.*" There is a curious phraseology to this statement which is well worth noting. Revelation is always based on relationship. My wife knows my bank account number; she has free access to my account at any time. That access is based on our relationship. Moses was shown the ways of God, but the people of Israel saw only his deeds. Moses had access to the LORD's inner sanctum. He met regularly with God in the Tent of Meeting. He was privy to the counsel of the LORD. That relationship resulted in a far greater revelation of God's plans and purposes.

Do you want a greater revelation of God's plan and purpose for your life? Seek to know God better. Spend time with Him. David brought the Ark of the Covenant to Jerusalem for that very reason. He wanted to be close to God, to spend time with Him daily, and to praise and worship Him freely. Relationship is always the wellspring of all revelation. It is while we are in God's presence that we discover the mind of Christ.

David certainly discovered the very nature of God. He discovered that "*... the* LORD *is compassionate and gracious, slow to anger, abounding in love.*" No sentence in the entire Bible captures the pure essence of God quite as fully as this one. It should be indelibly written on our hearts and minds. David could pen these words because he experienced them. He experienced God's boundless grace; he was an object of the LORD's great compassion.

When you live life in the extreme as David did, you are capable of both extreme failure and extreme success. You can bring down Goliath to the glory of God, and you can bring down an innocent man, Uriah the Hittite, to satisfy your selfish fleshly cravings. We are capable of both. The same testosterone-fuelled spirit of conquest undergirds both endeavors: one is inspired by God, the other reeks of hell's sulfur.

Men are divinely engineered to conquer. We despise wimps. The real test is whether our conquests are directed by the Spirit of God, or by Satan working through our base desires. In God's eyes, David was both an extreme success and an extreme failure. That is why David needed an extreme God—extremely loving, extremely patient and, above all, extremely forgiving. The LORD *is* an extremist.

The amazing thing about David is that he clung to God in both extremes—when he succeeded beyond his wildest dreams and when he failed spectacularly. In his success, David tapped into the amazing grace of God, the supernatural enablement of the LORD. In his moral failure, David found the extreme love and mercy of God.

So it is that David could pen these words about the LORD: *"He will not always accuse, nor will he harbor his anger forever; he does not treat us as our sins deserve or repay us according to our iniquities."*

David, the adulterer and murderer, penned those words. The extreme sinner found the God of extreme mercy. David's adultery with Bathsheba and his premeditated murder of Uriah meant that David deserved death. The law of the LORD prescribed it. But instead he received mercy, extreme mercy from an extreme God. He did not deserve God's goodness; we never do. A cross on a hill makes that abundantly clear.

"For as high as the heavens are above the earth, so great is his love for those that fear him, as far as the east is from the west, so far has he removed our transgressions from us."

David, the spectacular failure, found the LORD to be spectacularly loving. And this extreme sinner needed an extremely loving and forgiving God.

How far has God removed your sins from you? In the infinity of space, east never meets west. The cleansing is complete. The sin is gone. Forgiven. Forever gone in time, space, and eternity. Gone.

Totally forgiven means just that. What an extreme God!

> As a father has compassion on his children, so the LORD has compassion on those who fear him; for he knows how we are formed, he remembers that we are dust. As for man, his days are like grass, he flourishes like a flower of the field; the wind blows over it and it is gone, and its place remembers it no more.

There is a humble humanity to these words, a certain taste of Jesus in them. Jesus taught us to pray, "Our Father ..."

Did Jesus have these words of David in mind as He taught His disciples about His heavenly Father? Did David grasp the finite nature of his own earthly life as he contemplated the magnificent, infinite One? We certainly catch a glimpse of eternity in his words that follow:

"But from everlasting to everlasting the LORD's love is with those who fear him, and his righteousness with their children's children—with those who keep his covenant and remember to obey his precepts."

It is striking to note that the extreme forgiveness of the LORD does not produce a flippant, nonchalant attitude toward sin. It didn't in David, and shouldn't in us. Just the opposite is true. The extreme love of God for humanity gives birth within us to a hunger for right-eousness. The loved and forgiven yearn to obey the LORD of mercy.

Who would not fear and love such an extreme God? Who would not want to transfer the knowledge of this extreme LORD to the generations yet to come? I long to see my children's children loving and obeying this extremist God.

After all, I am forgiven.

Praise the LORD!

Bringing Life to the Psalms

1. Are you aware of any present-day Davids? Who are they? What can we learn from them?

2. David had a life of ups and downs, but throughout, he was faithful to the LORD and he finished well. Take time to read about the close of David's life in 1 Chronicles 28 – 29. What can you learn about finishing well from this biblical account?

3. Psalm 103 is filled with superlatives regarding the love of God. In many ways it has its New Testament parallel in Paul's prayer for the Ephesians. Take a moment to read that prayer in Ephesians 3:14-21.

4. Do you want a greater revelation of God's plan and purpose for your life? Seek to know God better. Spend time with Him this week. Be as purposeful in prayer, praise, and worship as David was.

5. Jesus came to announce and establish the Kingdom of God. In the first century, it burst upon the Roman world with power. Has it now turned into the Wimpdom of God? Has the church become effeminate? What can you do to make your church a place where men become Kingdom builders and true disciples of Christ?

The LORD Rules Over All

*The LORD has established his throne in heaven,
and his kingdom rules over all.
Praise the LORD, you his angels, you mighty
ones who do his bidding,
who obey his word.
Praise the LORD, all his heavenly hosts, you his
servants who do his will.
Praise the LORD, all his works everywhere in his
dominion.
Praise the LORD, O my soul.*

PSALM 103 IS A SANDWICH OR, IF you prefer, a big beefy hamburger. By that I mean this psalm begins with a personal call to praise the LORD and it ends, as we see from the passage above, with what amounts to a universal call to praise the

LORD. Between these calls to worship, we find a great big helping of God's goodness. In between we discover the reasons why we should be overflowing with praise to the LORD.

David experienced God's saving grace, goodness, love, and forgiveness over and over again. Consequently, his heart was full to bursting with praise. Herein is the "why" of praise: the reason for praise rests in God, not in us or our circumstances.

But Psalm 103 is not just a beefy hamburger. It is also an express train—a big steam locomotive. There is a distinct momentum to this psalm that can be missed by breaking it into sections. It begins with David addressing his soul. It would appear, at the start, to be a sluggish soul that is somewhat reluctant to praise God. But this reluctance begins to melt away as David recounts the LORD's great goodness. One by one, David declares the character qualities of the LORD. As each attribute is portrayed, David's sense of awe and his desire to praise God picks up momentum. By the end of this psalm, David's praise has become an express train, loaded with divine purpose and headed full speed for glory!

His final call to worship in the above stanza is a great cry for all to get aboard this express train of praise. Now with a full head of steam, in exultant praise, I can hear him shouting, "Hop on board, one and all! Praise the LORD! We are heaven bound!"

Many see praise and worship as a purely cathartic response to the manifest goodness of God. Something good happens to us. Unexpectedly, we get a thousand-dollar check in the mail. Quite naturally our response is praise to God.

For many people, praise to God never progresses beyond this natural, cathartic level. If God does not bless, no praise is forthcoming. Our praise for the LORD becomes, or simply remains, circumstance dependent. But that was not the case with David. His praise extended beyond simple catharsis. He taught his soul to praise the LORD in all circumstances. True biblical praise and worship is, after all, a spiritual exercise, a discipline we grow in, just as we grow in the discipline of prayer.

The LORD, the object of our praise, does not change with our circumstances. He is forever the same. *"Jesus Christ is the same yesterday and today and forever"* (Hebrews 13:8). He is constant; hence our praise and worship of Him should be constant, unaffected by weather conditions, world events, the gyrations of the stock market, our mood swings, or our personal situation.

Of course, this constancy in praise is something against which the natural man simply rebels. Our world needs to be right in order for us to praise God aright, or so we reason. The only problem with this logic is that the world has never been right since the Fall. Death, disease, war, and misery have been raining down on the children of Adam since willful disobedience to God first took root among us. And this is one weather forecast for all humanity that is not about to change—not until Christ returns.

If we are waiting for a perfect world before we lift our voices in praise to God, we will never praise Him. In fact, if our eyes are on the world or on ourselves, there will always be grounds to withhold our praise. But the whole purpose of praise and worship is to lift up our eyes. We desperately need to get our eyes off ourselves, off the world, and onto God our Maker.

Martin Rinkart was a man who could be forgiven for cursing God. Pastor Rinkart (1586–1649) was caught up in the horrors of the Thirty Years' War. For a full year, his hometown, Eilenburg in Saxony, was besieged as war raged round about. The triple scourge of war, disease, and famine ravaged the community. Death was everywhere. The walled city was swamped by destitute refugees. Three times it was overrun by pillaging armies. As the crises worsened, Rinkart's pastoral colleagues succumbed to the plague and only he was left to conduct funerals. In the horrific year, 1637, he conducted more than 4,000 funerals, as many as fifty in a single day. One of those funerals was for his own dear wife. But rather than cursing his Creator or withholding worship, he composed the ageless hymn of praise, *Now Thank we all our God.* Read his words of praise:

> *Now thank we all our God*
> *With heart and hands and voices,*
> *Who wondrous things hath done,*
> *In whom His world rejoices;*
> *Who from our mothers' arms,*
> *Hath blessed us on our way*
> *With countless gifts of love,*
> *And still is ours today.*

Martin Rinkart did not live in a perfect world, but his eyes saw beyond the death and destruction that lay before him. He lifted his eyes above the world and beyond himself. When he did, he beheld God. He saw Him as LORD over all, a God to be thanked and praised for countless gifts of love. In the midst of the most desperate situation imaginable, Pastor Rinkart fixed his gaze on the LORD his Maker. Then this humble pastor did a most remarkable thing—a Spirit-directed thing. He raised his voice in praise to God.

In a world run amok, all too often the first casualty is our faith in God. The chaos of disaster leads us to question the very existence of God. The God of order and control would not—should not—unleash tsunamis of war and disease on this world. We reason, "What kind of God is this? Why would an all-powerful god permit this? Why would he not spare those dear to me?"

But Martin Rinkart, the hymnist, and David, the psalmist, knew the true God—the God who exists beyond our narrow definitions of order and control. Both these men knew the LORD of all the earth. In Psalm 103, David declares, *"The LORD has established his throne in heaven, and his kingdom rules over all."*

That divine rule and that eternal kingdom truly encompass all—including disasters. Yes, He is LORD over disasters too—over war, hurricanes, floods, and droughts. He is LORD over both feasts and famines, joys and sorrows. He is LORD of all.

This declaration of God's kingdom rule collides head-on with my own preconceived notions of how the world should be. In my world, death should never steal a friend away. In my world, abundance should be a preordained right. In my world, sickness should have no foothold and cancer should hold no sway. In my world, all stories should have happy endings.

I want an ideal world like that. I want the real world to conform to my desired ends. When God does not meekly comply by granting me my ideal vision of the world, I stamp my foot and shake my fist at Him. In reality, when I do that I am announcing that I want to be God. I want to be LORD. A refusal to bow in worship before God is a declaration of my desire to be the sole ruler of my life and the creator of my own world apart from God.

In a world run amok, Martin Rinkart did not stamp his foot and shake his fist at God; he lifted his voice in praise. Praise to God in the midst of tragedy aligns us afresh with the LORD of the universe. It reestablishes and reasserts His direct rule over us. Along with David we declare, *"The LORD has established his throne in heaven, and his kingdom rules over all."*

God in His wisdom has not given me my ideal world. He has given me His world—the real world—where sorrow mingles with joy, where the curse and the blessing of Eden coexist, and where life and death dance nimbly together.

Prayer is my attempt before God to change this present world. This world is in desperate need of change. God and I are in agreement on that point. That's why He sent His Son. The world can be changed by God through prayer. What an astonishing truth! My prayers can change the world. God can, as a consequence of my prayers, intervene and stunningly alter the natural course of events. I have seen Him do astonishing miracles. He is, after all, who He says He is. He is LORD.

But if God does not intervene, if my prayers are not answered, if no miracle comes, He is still LORD. He is still to be praised. This inalterable fact remains, *"The LORD has established his throne in heaven, and his kingdom rules over all."*

After 4,000 funerals and after his hopes and dreams lay buried, for Martin Rinkart, God was still God. He was still LORD over all. He was still worthy of all praise and so Pastor Rinkart wrote:

> *O may this bounteous God,*
> *Through all our life be near us,*
> *With ever joyful hearts*
> *And blessed peace to cheer us;*
> *And keep us in his grace,*
> *And guide us when perplexed,*
> *And free us from all ills*
> *In this world and the next.*[5]

How shallow is your praise? Do you believe your world needs to be right before you praise God? Lift up your eyes for a moment. Lift them to the One who was lifted up for you. Lift your eyes to the Father who did not spare His Son, but sent Him into a messed-up world to die upon a cross. Fix your eyes on Him, the bloodied fount of redemption. Fix your eyes on the One who said, *"I am the way and the truth and the life"* (John 14:6).

Then lift your voice in praise to God.

How shallow is your praise? Do you believe you need to feel

---

[5] *Now Thank We All Our God*, Words by Martin Rinkart (1586–1649), 1636 Translated by Catherine Winkworth (1827–1878), 1858 MIDI: Nun danket alle Gott (later form of melody by Johann Cruger, 1598–1662).

right in order to praise right? After all, wouldn't we be hypocritical if we were outwardly exuberant in praise to God, but our heart was not in it? In this instance, when we speak of our heart, we really mean our feelings. But if we see praise as a biblical command, our feelings are inconsequential. We are to praise God regardless of our feelings. Feelings come and go, but the goodness of God stands secure and unchanging.

As residents of North America, we are a pampered lot. We live in affluence, materially rich, but mired in deep spiritual poverty. Gratification must be instant. Personal comfort trumps all other considerations. What do we know of hardship? In this sheltered atmosphere, praise for God grows like a spindly hothouse plant. Untested by hardship or the cold winds of adversity, our faith lacks depth. Our worship remains shallow.

If the music isn't right on Sunday, we are incapable of praise. What an outrageous affront to God! True worship is so much more than a lip-synched ditty. It goes deeper. It flows higher. It breaks through our emotional indifference and reaches the heart of God.

The deepest praise is sacrificial. It floats heavenward on a sea of suffering. It confounds all logic and rises above whim or emotion.

"Through Jesus, therefore, let us continually offer to God a sacrifice of praise—the fruit of lips that confess his name" (Hebrews 13:15).

True worship is born of the Spirit. Along with David, it invites all of heaven—all of creation—to join in the chorus of praise.

> *Praise the LORD you his angels, you mighty ones who do his bidding, who obey his word. Praise the LORD all his heavenly hosts, you his servants who do his will. Praise the LORD, all his works everywhere in his dominion. Praise the LORD, O my soul!*

Bringing Life to the Psalms

1. What does it mean to offer a sacrifice of praise? Have you faced times of hardship when you found it difficult to praise God? Were you able to offer praise?

2. Read a biographical portrait of Martin Rinkart. There are several Internet sites that provide a closer look at this man who knew how to praise God through adversity.

3. Read or sing Rinkart's great hymn, *Now Thank We All Our God.* It's a wonderful way to set free the wellspring of praise within you.

4. Reread Psalm 103. Is it a hamburger, an express train, or both? Can you think of another metaphor that helps our minds to capture the magnificence of this psalm? What is God saying to you as you read this psalm?

The Name of the LORD

Praise the LORD.
Praise, O servants of the LORD,
praise the name of the LORD.
Let the name of the LORD be praised,
both now and forevermore.
From the rising of the sun to the place where
it sets,
the name of the LORD is to be praised.

ANOTHER CHRISTMAS HAS COME
and gone. I am sitting across from our family Christmas tree as I write
this chapter. Snow is gently falling outside my living room window. It's
that relaxing time of year, the festive interlude between Christmas

Day and New Year's Day. It's a time to get my spiritual battery recharged, before the onslaught of the work routine returns along with the coming of a new year. As long as I can avoid big box stores and shopping malls, it's a peaceful time. I can spend extra time with the LORD and with family.

Praise the LORD!

Yes, praise the LORD for those relaxing times, when the pace of life slows down. We live in a rushed world, where quiet times and silent moments get crowded to the margins of our existence.

Silence? Silence is a rare experience in our rapid-fire, entertainment-hyped world. I wonder if *Silent Night* is such a popular carol because silence is a commodity we rarely experience but inwardly long for?

The people of the ancient world knew silence. It surrounded them like a huge, comforting blanket. They did not awaken to the blare of the radio or the din of urban traffic. Even so, they purposefully set apart times to get away and seek the LORD. Even the Son of God needed those times. After feeding the five thousand, Jesus did not throw a party with His disciples to celebrate His miracle. No, we read that *"he went up on a mountainside by himself to pray"* (Matthew 14:23).

Jesus longed to commune with his Father. He needed silent nights for that. He needed alone times.

How about you? If Jesus needed those quiet times—alone with God times—I know I most certainly do. And the starting point for any meaningful time with the LORD is the point of praise. We are to *"enter his gates with thanksgiving and his courts with praise; [to] give thanks and praise his name"* (Psalm 100:4).

That is precisely how Psalm 113 begins. It starts with praise:

> *Praise the LORD. Praise, O servants of the LORD,*
> *praise the name of the LORD. Let the name of the*

LORD *be praised, both now and forevermore.*
From the rising of the sun to the place where it
sets, the name of the LORD *is to be praised.*

And who precisely are we to praise? In both Psalm 100 and Psalm 113, the admonition is crystal clear. We are to praise the name of the LORD. *"Shout for joy to the* LORD, *all the earth. Worship the* LORD *with gladness; come before him with joyful songs"* (Psalm 100:1–2).

It must be noted that the psalmist did not instruct us to praise the name of the Lord. He instructed us to praise the name of the LORD. Did you catch the distinction? There is a huge difference between the words *Lord* and LORD that we can easily skip over or dismiss.

With enough money and influence, almost anyone can become a lord—a British lord. Conrad Black, the newspaper baron, renounced his Canadian citizenship in order to become Lord Black of Crossharbour. Along with the title of lord comes a seat in the House of Lords in the British Parliament.

In this world there are many lords and would-be lords, but there is only one LORD. The LORD is the Lord of both the heavens and the earth. His kingdom reign has no beginning or end; it is eternal. His dominion knows no bounds. The LORD is truly Lord of all, including Crossharbour. His seat, the throne of the universe, lies beyond the highest heavens. His glory never ceases. It is never tarnished by scandal, never debauched by sin. He is without peer. He is the LORD of lords.

In most Bible translations the word LORD is actually a kind of acronym. The capitalized letters of the word LORD stand for the Divine Name, the Hebrew language "Tetragrammaton." The Hebrews considered the Name too sacred to be spoken—a practice which is still followed among worshipping Jews today. An exact transliteration of the Hebrew word for LORD into English would yield YHWH. Biblical scholars and experts in linguistics agree that with the addition of Hebrew vowel markers, this word would most likely be pronounced Yahweh. However, instead of speaking out the word Yahweh, Hebrew speakers would substitute the word *Adonai*, which means Lord. The name Yahweh was deemed too holy to be spoken by human lips. In deference to this tradition, and in honor of the sacred Name, modern translators have substituted the capitalized word LORD for YHWH.

Accordingly, the opening verses of Psalm 113 could also be rendered thus:

> *Praise YHWH! Praise, O servants of YHWH, praise the name of YHWH. Let the name of YHWH be praised, both now and forevermore. From the rising of the sun to the place where it sets, the name of YHWH is to be praised.*

How sacred is the name of the LORD to you? Does it roll off your tongue with little meaning, or in your mind and heart is it truly linked to the LORD of lords? Do you reverence His name as His chosen people do? His glory and His character are resident within His name, the sacred name of the LORD. Do you speak His name thoughtlessly?

This is, after all, the LORD whose name means I AM. He is the self-existent One, without beginning or end. He is the One who, when asked, declared His identity to Moses. *"God said to Moses, 'I AM WHO I AM. This is what you are to say to the Israelites: I AM has sent me to you'"* (Exodus 3:14).

It was this same Moses who came down Mount Sinai with the Ten Commandments etched on tablets of stone. One of those commands reads as follows: *"You shall not misuse the name of the LORD your God, for the LORD will not hold anyone guiltless who misuses his name"* (Exodus 20:7).

In the spirit realm, invocation is a power-laden term. To invoke someone's name simply means to give voice to that name. If you call out my name in a public gathering, you will quickly get my attention. Our ears are always tuned to hear our own name. I may be surrounded by indecipherable babble, but toss my name into the midst of that babble and I'll pick up my ears every time. Not only that—I'll come right over to find out what is being said about me. That is the power of invocation.

The same is true in the spirit realm. We even have a common saying to express this truth, "Speak of the Devil, and he'll show up."

If the power of invocation works with me, and it works with the Devil who is not omnipresent, then you can be absolutely certain that it works with the name of the LORD. Speak His name, and He will show up. In Psalm 34, David declares, *The eyes of the LORD are on the righteous and his ears are attentive to their cry.* David goes on to assert, *"The righteous cry out, and the LORD hears them; he delivers them from all their troubles"* (Psalm 34:15, 17).

The prophet Joel takes this truth one step further. While speaking of the troubled times before the LORD's return, he states, *"And everyone who calls on the name of the LORD will be saved"* (Joel 2:32).

In the midst of this world's babble, the LORD will always hear His name. He will show up. He will eavesdrop on every conversation when His name is mentioned. He will hear every whispered prayer. He will stop by every meal where grace is spoken. He will be by your side, even when death comes knocking. Just speak His name.

This is the power of invocation; it is the power resident in His name—the name of the LORD. It behooves us to use His name aright, not flippantly or as swear word. That is the Devil's game, and we play on his side when we besmirch or desecrate the holy name. I have no time or respect for those who misuse my name. Why would we expect the LORD Almighty to be any different?

But my ears are always open to praise. It puts a smile on my face. Would it be any different with the LORD? When we gather to praise the LORD, He will be present at the mention of His name. According to the footnote, Psalm 22:3 could also be translated to read, *"Yet you are holy, enthroned on the praises of Israel."*

I rather like the thought of making a place for the LORD among us. As we praise His name, He comes to be with us. He pulls up a chair and sits with us for a time. He is enthroned on our praise. Through our praise we make room for Him in our lives. Our praises, whether spoken or sung, form an open invitation to Him. It is as though we are saying, "LORD, come sit with us for a while. Come be enthroned among us."

So let His praise resound. *"Let the name of the LORD be praised, both now and forevermore."*

Our praises join with others to form a continuum of praise for the LORD. It is a continuum that stretches back to the dawn of time. Can you imagine Adam waking to a beautiful dawn on that first morning in the Garden of Eden? He stretches, and then in thanksgiving he raises his hands and his voice in praise to his Creator. We join our voices with Adam and Eve, our first parents, when we too praise our Creator. We join our voices in praise with Abraham, the father of all who are justified by faith. We join with David, who danced before the LORD with all his might in celebration of the mercy of God. We blend our praise with the prophet Isaiah, who saw the LORD high and exalted, with six-winged seraphs calling out, *"Holy, holy, holy is the LORD Almighty; the whole earth is full of his glory"* (Isaiah 6:3).

This eternal praise continuum extends back to include all the heavenly hosts from before the earth took form. It encompasses all of creation both past and present, the birds, the animals, and the sea creatures. It draws all of life into worship. *"Let everything that has breath praise the LORD"* (Psalm 150:6).

It includes the women Jesus met on the best morning since creation—resurrection morning. Jesus greeted them, and then these women *"came to him, clasped his feet and worshiped him"* (Matthew 28:9).

Oh, what a moment of praise! It still resounds. It will resound throughout history.

We are united in our praise with Thomas, who touched the wounds of the living Christ. Then overwhelmed, he exclaimed in humble worship, *"My Lord and my God!"* (John 20:28).

Our praise for the LORD unites with the praises of the martyrs throughout the ages. It echoes from the catacombs and the arches of the Roman Coliseum, through the Middle Ages and the Reformation, right onto the back pages of today's newspaper. We bow our knees in unison with all these who suffer for His name. We bow with them in worship. We bow to the King of kings and the Lord of lords.

In praise to the LORD, we join with Handel to declare that our Messiah has come and His Kingdom reign will never cease. Praise the LORD! Strike up the chorus. Hallelujah! Along with Beethoven we declare that Jesus is our Ode to Joy.

The glory of His name is not bound by the confines of time and place. It supersedes national boundaries. The LORD who parted the Red Sea also parted the Iron Curtain. He took His own special sledgehammer to the Berlin Wall. He is LORD of the nations, whether they acknowledge Him or not.

In the face of Christ we see the LORD. In His name we have redemption. The apostle Paul declares, *"God exalted him to the highest place and gave him the name that is above every name, that at the name of Jesus every knee should bow, in heaven and on earth and under the earth, and every tongue confess that Jesus Christ is Lord, to the glory of God the Father"* (Philippians 2:9–11).

Now we join with the psalmist and declare, *"From the rising of the sun to the place where it sets, the name of the* LORD *is to be praised."*

Yes, praise the LORD! Praise His name. Praise deity clothed in humanity, who in the temple courts confessed His name, *"I tell you the truth … before Abraham was born, I AM!"* (John 8:58).

On bended knee we confess, "Jesus Christ is Lord."
Yes, He is LORD!

Bringing Life to the Psalms

1. Were you aware of the distinction between the words LORD and
Lord before you read this chapter? Does this knowledge affect your
use of the name of the LORD?

2. The great "I am" statements of Christ recorded in John's Gospel are
a direct link to Yahweh, who is the Great I AM. John's Gospel most
clearly portrays the deity of Christ. Take a moment to read Jesus'
bold confession of His deity in John 8:48–59.

3. We are instructed to pray in Jesus' name. Take a moment to read
afresh those instructions found in John 14:5–14.

4. Are you aware of the power of invocation? Be assured the LORD
has ears to hear and He will show up. He will honor His name.

The God who Stoops Down

The LORD is exalted over all the nations,
his glory above the heavens.
Who is like the LORD our God,
the One who sits enthroned on high,
who stoops down to look on the heavens and
the earth?
He raises the poor from the dust
and lifts the needy from the ash heap;
he seats them with princes,
with the princes of their people.
He settles the barren woman in her home
as the happy mother of children.
Praise the LORD.

YOU MIGHT HAVE A PICTURE OF
yourself like this. You know the kind. It is less than flattering. It provides a great view of your backside as you are bent over or, better yet, someone has caught you in the classic plumber position, with your

head under the sink and your opposite end in full view.

I know what to do with photos like that. I toss them in the garbage. I erase them from my hard drive. If I can wrestle the cellphone camera from the photographer, I will hit the delete button faster than the shutter speed for that priceless Kodak moment.

Who wants to embarrass him or herself and then keep the evidence for posterity? Apparently, God does. In fact, the LORD has been doing it since time began. Proof of this can be found right here in Psalm 113:

"The LORD is exalted over all the nations, his glory above the heavens. Who is like the LORD our God, the One who sits enthroned on high, who stoops down to look on the heavens and the earth?"

Who indeed? Why would the exalted One, the enthroned One, stoop down? How undignified! Doesn't the LORD know that kings and potentates don't bend over or stoop down? They certainly don't do that sort of thing in public—not where they can be seen by others. Rulers rule from the seat of authority. They sit; they don't stoop down.

But our God stoops down. If the truth be told, it is even worse than that.

The LORD doesn't just stoop down; He plays in the mud. He has been playing in the mud for years now, ever since He shaped us from the dust of the earth. I would go so far as to say that this behavior— this playing in the mud—has become an obsession with Him. It is a divine obsession. He just keeps right on doing it.

I'm not sure how the LORD justifies His behavior. From a perfectly logical point of view, it simply does not make sense. After all, I would hardly call the LORD's first experience with mud sculpture a glowing success. Sure, Adam looked handsome enough and Eve was pretty sweet, but that breath of life idea was a complete disaster.

And what thanks did God get for His efforts? Well, the dear little mud clods disobeyed Him. They disobeyed their Maker at the first opportunity, or so I've read. What a show of gratitude! But then, I suppose that's what you get for stooping down and playing in the mud. It goes to show what you can expect from quickened mud clods.

After that experience—that catastrophe run amuck—you would think the LORD would know better. He *should* know better by now. But no, not the LORD! He keeps right on going back to the mud holes. He insists on stooping down and rescuing these little, living, breathing dirt bags.

Take David for example. Let's call him exhibit A. But rather than listen to me go on about the LORD's absurd behavior, why not hear David's own testimony:

> I waited patiently for the LORD; he turned to me and heard my cry. He lifted me out of the slimy pit, out of the mud and the mire; he set my feet on a rock and gave me a place to stand. He put a new song in my mouth, a hymn of praise to our God. Many will see and fear and put their trust in the LORD (Psalm 40:1–3).

Well David, this is all fine and good for you to say. But remember, you're the one who got yourself into that mess—that mud and mire—in the first place. Have you given even a moment's thought to the LORD's dignity? I think not. He has a whole universe to rule, and there you are interrupting Him with your pathetic pleas. The LORD has to leave His contemplations, get off His kingly throne and rescue you—from a mud hole! I am sure God has better things to do than to chase after the likes of you.

And David, this new song of yours—this hymn of praise—let me give you some advice. Pull the plug on it. Why would you want to broadcast your own failings? Why would you want the world to see how dependent you are on the LORD? It is time to grow up. Learn to stand on your own two feet. This running to the LORD for everything has got to stop. Don't you realize He has a whole world to run?

Worst of all David, if you go ahead with this new song, it will turn out just as you say. Many will see how the LORD has rescued you. They will put their trust in the LORD. And what will happen then? Well, I'll tell you what will happen. Next thing you know, the LORD won't have a moment's rest. Every slime ball on the planet will be calling out to Him.

And exactly how will the LORD respond? Well, if past performance is any indicator, He will be right out there, big time. He will be pulling slime balls out of mud holes all over the world. Like I said earlier, it's an obsession—a divine obsession.

Take this psalm, Psalm 113, for an example. Have a look at this quote. Let's call it exhibit B.

> *He raises the poor from the dust and lifts the needy from the ash heap; he seats them with princes, with the princes of their people. He settles the barren woman in her home as the happy mother of children. Praise the LORD!*

Why doesn't He stay seated? Why doesn't the LORD just stay on the throne? Why does He insist on stooping down and getting His hands dirty? You can't possibly lift people out of dust and ashes without getting your hands dirty.

And why does the LORD keep elevating people? Doesn't He know that they are the source of all the problems in the world? If He must interact with humanity, He should at the very least pick His contacts more carefully. Why associate with the poor—the scum of the earth? Go for the cream of the crop. If the LORD is so high and mighty, why doesn't He stick with the high and mighty? He keeps diving below His rank—well below His rank.

To be honest with you, the LORD seems to be completely out of touch with how this messed up world operates. When it comes to the LORD, it's like we're dealing with some kind of heavenly dumpster diver. He keeps finding treasures in the trash.

But what I find most disturbing about this passage is the statement about the barren woman. Help the woman if You must, LORD, but turning her into the happy mother of children is a terrible mistake. I'm not sure we need more of these sniveling, whining, God-needing, God-dependent creatures. Things will only get worse with more of them around. The LORD will never have a moment's rest—not with them bawling around for help. I can see it all now—even more stooping, more bending over mud holes. He'll spend even more time saving the incompetent from themselves.

In reality, this obsession with creatures of dust and extracting them from mud holes has gone totally out of control. It has completely taken over the mind of the LORD. That's what obsessions do. How else can you explain what happened next?

He decided to have a Son by one of these daughters of earth. You might even say the LORD decided to become one of them. I know it's incredible, absolutely incredible. I call it a case of divine insanity.

And the poor woman He had this child by, what a mess He left her in! First of all, you would think that the LORD who *is exalted over all the nations, who sits enthroned on high*" would choose a partner of noble birth, but not the LORD. No, He chose some poor, humble servant girl at the bottom rung of society. Granted, Mary came from royal stock, but this lineage of David that you read about meant absolutely nothing in practical terms. It didn't put food on the table or clothes on her back, or boost her social status.

Yes, you heard right. Mary is from the thousand-year-old line of David—the same David the LORD pulled out of the mud and the mire, way back then. Not exactly a proud legacy, in my opinion.

So the LORD *"who sits enthroned on high"* got Mary pregnant and then He left her. He left her high and dry—stranded. He didn't even hang around to explain Himself. He let Mary do the talking. He let her explain this whole mess to Joseph, her fiancé.

"*Who is like the* LORD *our God?*" Who indeed?

To top off this public relations fiasco, this descent from the heavenly realm, we have the actual birth of the Son of God. What a botched, low-budget affair that was! Unbelievable! Born in a stable. The Son of God in a manger—a feeding trough for slobbering cows! Incredible.

When the LORD stoops down, He really stoops down!

The lack of coordination in this whole event simply defies description. Was any thought put into this at all? Why this last minute rush? Why have the baby born in Bethlehem? Why not Jerusalem, the holy city, the capital?

And then there's that disaster with the angels. As far as I'm concerned they showed up in the wrong place entirely. Why announce the Savior's birth to a few poor, lowlife shepherds? They have no influence, no means to spread the news beyond a small circle. I can only assume the lead angel somehow got his coordinates mixed up and landed in the wrong location.

The heavenly choir was a nice touch. Here at last was some pomp and ceremony—some razzle dazzle and celestial fireworks befitting the birth of a heaven-sent King. But it was all wasted on those shepherds. Like I said, it happened in the wrong place. The LORD would have had far more bang for His buck if the angels had put on their show over Jerusalem.

Then there are the magi. Nice try, wise guys. Too bad you arrived almost two years after the fact and your blundering ineptitude almost got the Son of God killed.

No, this whole experiment in cross-cultural communication—heaven to earth communication—did not start well. Is it any wonder that things went quickly downhill from there?

As for the Son of God, well, He is just like His Father—the very image of Him! He has the same character too. He's always hanging around with the bottom end of society, with the harlots, the tax collectors, the sinners. He does a lot of stooping down too, and He plays in the mud. He spit on the ground and made some mud once. He used it to heal a man born blind (John 9:1–12). And then there's that time He pardoned the adulteress. On that occasion, He stooped down and did a lot of writing in the dirt (John 8:1–11).

Does any of this sound familiar? Well, they are familiar all right. As I said, the Son is just like the Father, and the Father is just like the Son.

As for this divine obsession with creatures of dust—this divine insanity—what did it lead to? It led straight to the cross—the Son's death on the cross.

As I said, you can't possibly lift people out of dust and ashes without getting your hands dirty. Well, Jesus, God's Son, couldn't lift people out of dust and ashes without getting His hands bloody. He got His hands pierced. I guess that's what the LORD gets for stooping down and playing in the dirt.

How do you explain all this? There are some things we will never fully understand. I am sure that this is one of those things. We cannot fathom this—not in a million years.

They say love is an obsession—a case of temporary insanity. That is the only explanation I can think of for this outcome. He has a bad case of love. The LORD has a terminal case of love. And in His case, it has never stopped; He has never gotten over it. He fell in love with us from the first time He saw us—from the moment He formed us. "For God so loved the world that he gave his one and only Son" (John 3:16).

Still, I keep wondering, why would anyone stoop so low? Why would the One who sits enthroned on high stoop so low for me?

Bringing Life to the Psalms

1. Jesus' earthly family members were not numbered among the rich and famous of the land. Read James 5:1–6. Our Lord's brother had some strong words for the rich and powerful. In the struggles of life, with whom do you identify—the wealthy or the poor?

2. Do you stoop down? Plan an activity that aims to help the poor or the disadvantaged. What are you doing to help the orphan or the widow, whether next door or on the other side of the globe?

3. Read the account of Jesus healing the man born blind in John 9:1–12. Note the similarities with the creation of Adam recorded in Genesis 2:4–7.

4. Simply take some time to thank the LORD for His incomparable love. Verbalize your thanks to Him.

5. Reread all of Psalm 113. What is God speaking to your heart as you read this psalm?

The Timing of God

*When Israel came out of Egypt,
the house of Jacob from a people of foreign
tongue,
Judah became God's sanctuary,
Israel his dominion.
The sea looked and fled,
the Jordan turned back;
the mountains skipped like rams,
the hills like lambs.*

ALL DAY, I JUST WANTED TO GET
out. The park across the street beckoned. On sunny days it seems
only natural to want to get outside, at least for part of the day. In
January, sunny, warm days are a rarity in Ottawa and this particular

day was a real gem. There was no snow on the ground—an unheard of phenomenon for this part of the country—at what is normally the coldest time of year. The thermometer was on the plus side of the ledger and, from dawn onward, warm sunshine poured down. Best of all, this January gem had landed on the weekend.

But a variety of chores and obligations kept me indoors. Finally, at three thirty in the afternoon, I was able to escape the confines of our home. But it was too late. Only moments before I stepped outside, the sun disappeared behind a thick cloud. Within an hour it sank below the horizon. My much-anticipated sunlit stroll through the park never happened. Actually the stroll took place, but it transpired in an ever-deepening midwinter gloom.

Time works that way; it always works that way. If we don't seize the moment, the moment escapes, never to be recaptured. We can try to make amends or rearrange our schedule, but time is an unforgiving tyrant. It marches on; the sun sets. We will never have that day, hour, minute, or moment again. We seize it or lose it. We catch the sun's rays when it shines or we reap the gathering gloom.

Furthermore, events that occur in time can affect all of eternity. Catch the right moment and you change the course of the world. Seize the apex moment with God, and all of human history will be transformed. That familiar old maxim is true: timing is everything.

Here in Psalm 114 we find an apex moment. Moses seized that moment—the ideal instant in time—and as a consequence a nation was set free. Israel, the nation, was born in that apex moment.

"*When Israel came out of Egypt, the house of Jacob from a people of foreign tongue, Judah became God's sanctuary, Israel his dominion.*"

Moses was first summoned by God at the burning bush and, despite his hesitation, he responded to the LORD's call. His full obedience to that call resulted in his people's deliverance from the yoke of cruel oppression. There was a perfect timing—a divine timing—in all this. Deliverance did not come a moment too soon or arrive a moment too late. The LORD is always right on time.

We are the ones who are impatient, who miss the moment, who come too early or show up too late. Young Moses suffered from this problem too. His timing was off. He harbored ambitions of delivering his people. He wanted to rescue them. And why not? He saw their desperate need. He wanted to help. He was both a son of Pharaoh's daughter and a son of Israel. Moses bridged these two communities. Surely, as a man of position and influence raised in Pharaoh's household, he could use that influence to bring about change. But unfettered ambition can be impetuous. After murdering an Egyptian taskmaster, Moses fled in fear for his life.

Moses had jumped the gun. On his own strength, he had raced ahead of God. He was fuelled by good intentions, but his ill-conceived attempt at helping his people ended in disaster and disgrace. For forty years he lived as a guilt-ridden fugitive in the Desert of Sinai. His self-generated efforts were out of sync with God. Forty years is a long time. Sometimes it takes a long time to get right timing—to get into God's timing.

Finally, when the time was right, it was God who called Moses. Now, that is a strange reversal. Typically, we see a need and we then go and enlist God to help us rectify the situation. But here it was God who initiated the project. This rescue mission was the LORD's idea, and it would be done His way, on His timetable, under His leadership. The LORD made this perfectly clear in His introductory remarks to Moses at the burning bush. Speaking of the suffering Israelites, He said, "*I have come down to rescue them from the hand of the Egyptians and to bring them up out of that land into a good and spacious land, a land flowing with milk and honey*" (Exodus 3:8).

Unlike Moses' earlier clumsy attempt at national deliverance, this time it was solely the LORD's rescue mission. It was His project. Moses was invited to join the operation or he could sit on the sidelines.

The formerly-eager Moses almost chose the sidelines.

Take a moment to consider this. How many needs do you see? How many well-intentioned projects do you take on? Now ask yourself how many of these projects are first conceived in the heart of God? How many are initiated by Him? There is a vast difference between what is self-initiated and that which is God-initiated. Has the LORD summoned you to the burning bush? Or are you busy trying to enlist Him to your well-intentioned causes?

There is no room for personal ambition at the burning bush. Perhaps that was the reason for Moses' reluctance to sign on for this divine rescue mission. He had already tried and failed to bring deliverance, and now the LORD wanted him to take up the cause again. But this time Moses would not be in charge. The LORD would be calling all the plays. Personal pride would need to be sent to the sidelines.

I doubt that from among the descendants of Israel, the LORD could have found a more reluctant leader than Moses. For a full chapter and a half in the Book of Exodus, Moses is trying to wheedle his way out of this divine assignment. Finally we read: "*Moses begged, 'LORD, please send someone else to do it'*" (Exodus 4:13 CEV).

If I were Moses and the LORD had tapped me for this assignment, I too may have been reluctant. I might have had a few choice questions for the LORD. I think the first question would have been, "Where have You been for the last eighty years? It's nice for You to show up now, LORD, but this suffering has been going on for a very long time. My people have been whipped and mistreated and their babies have been tossed in the Nile. Where have You been, LORD? I think Your timing is off.

"And where were You, LORD, when I tried to get something going forty years ago? I could have used Your help back then. Now You show up forty years after the fact. Suddenly You're a convert to the cause—a latecomer. Welcome on board. But aside from Your heavenly status, I am not sure why You should be the One in charge of this Hebrew rescue mission."

These questions may be crudely put, but I suspect that below the surface they were percolating in Moses' mind. Fortunately for the Hebrews, I was not living in Moses' skin or they might still be stuck in the slime pits of Egypt.

But this was a different Moses than the rash young man who fled to the Sinai Desert forty years earlier. Perhaps it was time spent in the wilderness that liberated Moses from the tyranny of self. His personal agenda now lay buried under the shifting sands of time. Youthful self-assurance yielded at last to the Master's plan. When this hard earthen vessel finally removed his shoes in submission, the LORD could use him. The old Moses was dead—dead and buried. The new Moses—the Moses of the burning bush—was at last pliable in the Master's hands.

Forty years earlier, Moses had buried the Egyptian taskmaster beneath the sands of Egypt. Now the self-confident, I'll-do-it-myself Moses, the do-it-my-way Moses, was finally laid to rest beneath the desert sands of Sinai.

God is accustomed to using dead men. In fact it can be argued that they are His preferred instruments to accomplish His purpose in the world. Dead men don't take credit for the sovereign work of God. They don't swell with pride. Dead men don't argue with the Master over His chosen course of action. Dead men don't frighten easily. They don't shrink back when they are asked to do the impossible. Dead men don't give up when the going gets tough. Only dead men are fully in sync with God's timing.

God can use dead men. He did not use Abraham to become the father of the faithful until the apex moment—until Abraham was *"as good as dead … so from this one man … came descendants as numerous as the stars in the sky and as countless as the sand on the seashore"* (Hebrews 11:12).

Figuratively, Isaac, the son of promise, needed to die on the hill of sacrifice. Out of death came life—life in harmony with God. Jacob's grasping ambition died at Peniel. Joseph's dreams of glory died a thousand deaths before Israel and his sons bowed before the master of all of Egypt. When at last the strong arm of the flesh is dead and buried, there is room for the life of God to spring forth.

Headstrong, impetuous Peter needed to hear the third crow from the rooster before his heart broke. Only then was he fully ready to yield to the Master's touch. All his self-deceiving, self-aggrandizing ambition needed to die. His rancid, sinful nature was a stench in the very nostrils of God. The old man—the old egotistical Peter—was finally buried in the tomb right along with the body of Jesus. The old man was dead.

A new life awaited. The resurrected Jesus raised a new Peter to a new life—a life infused with the Spirit of God—a new life moving in God's perfect timing.

The grave is the best place for our bloated, sinful nature. It is always out of sync with God. It loves to dictate to God. The sinful nature, by its very nature, always feels it knows best. Like the pre-Pentecost Peter, our fleshly nature always believes it lives and moves in God's timing, but the only god it serves is the god of self.

No one understood this truth better than Paul the apostle. The old Paul—Saul of Tarsus—died on the road to Damascus. It was the new man—the new Paul—who wrote, "*I have been crucified with Christ and I no longer live, but Christ lives in me. The life I live in the body, I live by faith in the Son of God, who loved me and gave himself for me*" (Galatians 2:20).

When Moses died to himself and his worldly ambitions, God could use him for His eternal purpose. He became a vessel of honor, fit for the Master's use. The new Moses was infused with life and power from on high. It was the new Moses who led Israel out of Egypt.

The Timing of God

"When Israel came out of Egypt, the house of Jacob from a people of foreign tongue, Judah became God's sanctuary, Israel his dominion."

Have you come out of Egypt? Have you left the world and its enticements behind? Or are you still under pharaoh's jurisdiction, within Satan's domain? Are you a slave to the same old taskmasters? Have you crossed the Red Sea? In 1 Corinthians 10, Paul likens this passing through the sea to Christian baptism.

> *Or don't you know that all of us who were baptized into Christ Jesus were baptized into his death? We were therefore buried with him through baptism into death in order that, just as Christ was raised from the dead through the glory of the Father, we too may live a new life* (Romans 6:3–4).

When we come out of Egypt, God can come in. When the old man is dead and buried, the new life of Christ can be formed within us. When we have crossed the sea, our hearts become God's sanctuary, His habitation. We have renounced the world and its ways; we are now citizens in His dominion. When God comes in, everything changes.

"When ... Judah became God's sanctuary, Israel his dominion ... the sea looked and fled, the Jordan turned back; the mountains skipped like rams, the hills like lambs."

When God is present He changes everything. When our time is aligned with God's time, we are in the apex moment. Anything is possible. The seas flee—the sea of worry, the sea of doubt, the sea of guilt. They all flee away at the presence of the LORD. Mountains of heartache and trouble begin to skip away. They skip right out of sight. The God of the impossible casts them into the heart of the sea.

When God is present my needs are met; God's purpose is accomplished. There is joy. I am God's dwelling place—His sanctuary. He has dominion here. The old, rancid, sinful man is dead—dead and buried. Christ has arisen in me. I am in God's timing. It is as Jesus says, *"everything is possible for him who believes"* (Mark 9:23).

The Son is shining. The LORD is here.

Bringing Life to the Psalms

1. Have there been instances in your life where you have caught the apex moment with God? Reflect back on those times. Were there preconditions of the heart or your attitude that brought you into right timing with God? What is the role of God's sovereign grace during such times?

2. Many believers have not been baptized. Have you buried the old man—your sinful nature—through baptism? Have you been resurrected with Christ to a new life? Are you still struggling with sin? Baptism can act as a clear break with the old life. Take time to read Romans 6:1–14. New life begins on the other side of the sea.

3. Are you trying to enlist God to your well-intentioned causes? Have you taken on tasks without hearing from God first? Examine your life in the light of God's calling. Weed out what has not been planted by God. We are all called to fulfill God's purpose for our lives. Remember, if the LORD is giving you an assignment, He will direct and empower you. It may be your assignment, but it will always be His project—His mission. Be sure to do it His way.

The Miraculous Conundrum

Why was it, O sea, that you fled,
O Jordan, that you turned back,
you mountains, that you skipped like rams,
you hills, like lambs?
Tremble, O earth, at the presence of the LORD,
at the presence of the God of Jacob,
who turned the rock into a pool,
the hard rock into springs of water.

"WHY, DADDY? WHY?" A FOUR-
year-old's favorite question is, "Why?"

And why wouldn't it be? A four-year-old is living in the age of discovery. Everything is new. Everything is calling out to be discovered.

Exploration is the activity of the day. And always the question asked is, "Why?"

"Why is the sky blue? Why do girls wear dresses? Why did that egg break? Why?"

Here in Psalm 114, the psalmist has some *why* questions as well. "Why did the sea flee? Why did the Jordan River turn back? Why did those mountains and hills seem to skip and dance? Why?"

Why, indeed?

The answer, of course, is because of the jaw-dropping, eye-popping, heart-stopping power of God. He caused the sea to flee. He caused the Jordan to turn back. He caused mountains and hills to skip about and frolic like yearling lambs set free from the stall. What an awesome display!

What an awesome God!

Psalm 114 is all about the overwhelming power of God. It is a grand portrayal of the pivotal event in the Old Testament Scriptures. Here, within a few short verses, we catch a panoramic view of God's might on display, starting with Israel's escape from Egypt and ending with their arrival in the Promised Land. Our miracle-working God puts on a magnificent show. What an exhibition!

In the preview to this main event, the LORD, the God of Jacob, humiliated the gods of Egypt. Ten plagues devastated the land. The Nile turned to blood. The source of life for the nation became a stench—a source of death. Every plague crippled the pride of Egypt. Each one struck down a ruler of darkness from the nation's demonic pantheon. The plagues left no doubt as to who was in charge—who was the Lord over Egypt. The LORD God was Lord. Pharaoh and his wizards were powerless before this wonder-working God of Israel.

But the LORD did not finish with the ten plagues. This was only the preliminary round—the warm-up. The main event was still to come.

With Pharaoh's army in hot pursuit, Moses stretched out his staff and the sea fled. A path was opened through the deep, and the children of Israel made good their escape. When the army of Pharaoh continued to chase them across the seabed, the LORD threw them into confusion.

> *The water flowed back and covered the chariots and horsemen—the entire army of Pharaoh that had followed the Israelites into the sea. Not one of them survived. But the Israelites went through the sea on dry ground, with a wall of water on their right and on their left* (Exodus 14:28–29).

What an awesome display of power! Aside from the miracle of creation, this Old Testament miracle is viewed as the measuring rod—the gold standard—by which all other supernatural events are compared. In the Hebrew Scriptures, this event has no comparison; it is unparalleled. The whole nation saw this. They experienced this supernatural phenomenon. God confounded nature. Water formed a wall. The Almighty suspended what we call normal.

"*Why was it, O sea, that you fled?*"

The immediate answer to this question is simple, yet profound. The sea fled because of the power of God. In exultation Moses boasts,

> *Your right hand, O LORD, was majestic in power. Your right hand, O LORD, shattered the enemy. By the blast of your nostrils the waters piled up. The surging waters stood firm like a wall; the deep waters congealed in the heart of the sea. Who among the gods is like you, O LORD? Who is like you—majestic in holiness, awesome in glory, working wonders?* (Exodus 15:6, 8, 11).

But why did the miracle-working LORD make the sea flee? Was it simply to display His awe-inspiring power? Was it simply to create a bit of excitement among the million or more mortals who were eye-witnesses to this divine wonder?

In the Exodus account, the reason for this miraculous intervention is stated very clearly. Here, then, is the reason for this display of raw power:

> *That day the LORD saved Israel from the hand of the Egyptians, and Israel saw the Egyptians lying dead on the shore. And when the Israelites saw the great power the LORD displayed against the Egyptians, the people feared the LORD and put their trust in him and in Moses his servant* (Exodus 14:30–31).

This power display had one primary purpose. That purpose was salvation. The LORD wanted to save people—His covenant people—from the vicious clutches of oppression and tyranny. In short, the LORD works wonders so that He can save people—so He can bring them into His Kingdom—so they can escape the sin systems of this world and come under His loving rule.

So why did the sea flee? The LORD sent the sea fleeing so that He could save people.

But from the above passage in Exodus we can see that this miraculous intervention had two secondary effects. It caused people to stand in awe of the LORD, and it prompted them to put their trust in Him and His servant Moses. Suddenly the LORD had everyone's attention. It was impossible to deny the existence of this wonder-working God. Everyone in Israel saw and experienced this fear-prompting miracle. Furthermore, for every Israelite, the message in the miracle was crystal clear: "God is all-powerful. And this awe-evoking God truly cares about me. The LORD cared so much that, for a brief time, He suspended the laws of nature so that I could walk free."

What an awesome God! What a loving God! Is it any wonder then that the people put their trust in the LORD? They saw His divine character displayed. They were not just witnesses to His power; they were recipients of His love and mercy. God intervened into the affairs of a nation, Egypt, the ancient superpower, in order to bring His covenant people to the point of freedom. Then God intervened into the course of nature. He parted the sea to bring them to full liberty. What a deliverance! What a wonderful God!

"Why was it, O sea, that you fled, O Jordan, that you turned back, you mountains, that you skipped like rams, you hills, like lambs?"

On the day of their deliverance, for the common Hebrew, the answer to this question would have read something like this: "God worked wonders to save me. He made the sea flee just for me. That's why all this happened!"

That was the testimony of every slave who walked out of Egypt. And that same God works wonders today for the same reason—to save people and to bring them *"out of darkness into his marvelous light"* (1 Peter 2:9 CEV).

God works wonders. He works wonders today. But for me, there was a time when this miracle-working power of God was a huge stumbling block. For some people, faith seems to come easily or naturally. They read God's Word and readily believe it; they hear the preacher and believe the message he brings. But just the opposite was true for me as a young person. I was born with the mind of a skeptic. Reading biblical accounts of miracles did not inspire faith. These stories raised all kinds of questions and doubts. If there was one disciple I could identify with, it was Thomas. We had a similar world view.

You say God works miracles. Don't tell me—show me. That was my attitude. Though I had read the entire Bible by age eleven, I had a difficult time believing it. It simply did not align with the world as I saw and experienced it. Miracles did not occur in my world. Why should I believe they happened two thousand years ago? That was my line of reasoning in my teen years, and even now I see it as a perfectly logical position for an unbeliever to take.

When I talked to adults or church leaders about this question of miracles, they would brush off my doubts with a blithe remark about how miracles happened back then, in Bible times, but they did not happen anymore. This did nothing to set my skeptic's mind at ease. If miracles happened then, why didn't they happen now? If God never changes and if "*Jesus Christ is the same yesterday and today and forever*" (Hebrews 13:8), then it logically follows that the supernatural should be happening today. Unless, of course, the biblical miracles never happened in the first place.

I found myself in a miraculous conundrum. Did they happen or did they not? Should I believe the Bible or not? I wavered on this question for quite some time. In the end I resolved to believe, not because of evidence but because of love. I found the love of Christ as displayed on the cross too compelling, too overwhelming, to walk away from. I decided to believe because I loved the story of His great love. He gripped me at the cross. With nail-pinned hands, He took hold of me. I decided to believe.

In my teen years, the decision was finally made. I would follow Him, but the miraculous conundrum remained. The dispensational position on miracles made no sense to me. Why would miracles take place back then, but not now? Why? Why indeed?

We settle on second best if our faith rests solely on a decision. Decisions can change. Doubts can assail. The human mind is fickle, easily swayed by this or that argument. Inwardly I longed for a more firm foundation, one based on hard evidence and a rock-solid conviction. There is a substantial difference between believing and knowing. I longed to know God, not just believe in His existence.

Fortunately, we serve a living God who responds to the cry of our heart. If we seek after Him, He will respond. We have the sure promise of His word on that point.

"'You will seek me and find me when you seek me with all your heart. I will be found by you' declares the LORD" (Jeremiah 29:13–14).

And when we find the LORD, we find the God of power. The LORD responded to Jeremiah's questioning mind with this statement: *"I am the LORD, the God of all mankind. Is anything too hard for me?"* (Jeremiah 32:27).

Of course, nothing is too hard for the LORD. He can send the sea fleeing. If you are earnest in seeking Him and you want evidence of His existence, He will supply it. If in humility you seek a demonstration of His power, He is not weak. He will answer. In fact, He longs to fill His disciples with power—power that will strengthen our witness and bring others to salvation. Again we have Jesus' sure promise on that point:

> *But you will receive power when the Holy Spirit comes on you; and you will be my witnesses in Jerusalem, and all Judea and Samaria, and to the ends of the earth* (Acts 1:8).

The miracle-working power of God resides in the Holy Spirit. When as a young man I experienced a personal Pentecost, something very transformational happened inside me. In an instant I moved from believing in God to knowing God. For me, the evidence was in and a rock-solid conviction stood where my uncertain faith had formerly rested. I knew Jesus was alive. He sent His Spirit to affirm my faith.

The wonder-working power of God will do that. Doubters are silenced when God shows up. And yes, miracles have followed. On several occasions I have experienced divine healing, supernatural guidance, and best of all, I have been empowered to be His witness. The miracle of salvation has come to others. And this miracle-working God is not finished yet. What He began in Egypt He will complete in the Promised Land. As He turned back the Jordan for Israel, He will turn back the Jordan for me as well. He welcomes His people home. He is my provision and my provider for the journey, even as He was for Israel, and He will be your provision and your provider as well.

Tremble, O earth, at the presence of the LORD, *at the presence of the God of Jacob, who turned the rock into a pool, the hard rock into springs of water.*

Over the years, this bit of earth in human skin has had many occasions to tremble before the presence of the LORD. He is my provision for the journey even when the way is hard. By His Holy Spirit, He turns the barren rock into pools of refreshing. In the desert, He is my spring of living water.

Even today Jesus calls out, *"'If anyone is thirsty, let him come to me and drink. Whoever believes in me, as the Scripture has said, streams of living water will flow from within him.' By this he meant the Spirit, whom those who believed in him were later to receive"* (John 7:37–39).

Jesus the miracle worker calls us to the source of power. Now what about you? What sea lies before you, blocking your way? Does your God still work miracles? Let's watch that sea flee.

Bringing Life to the Psalms

1. God affirms our faith in Him with signs following. Read Mark 16:14–20. Have you experienced God's miracle-working power in your life? Have you seen it in others? Many believers have a strong faith without experiencing signs and wonders, yet others will not believe in God unless the miraculous occurs. How do you account for this difference?

2. *"Now to each one the manifestation of the Spirit is given for the common good"* (1 Corinthians 12:7). How has God manifested the Holy Spirit's presence in your life?

3. Is your faith decision-based or conviction-based? Are you convinced in your faith, or do you still experience doubts? Remember, God loves skeptics too. Have you experienced a transition from believing to knowing? Is this a valid way to look at the faith journey?

4. Reread Psalm 114. What is God saying to you by His Spirit through this psalm?

Pure by Your Word

Beth

How can a young man keep his way pure?
By living according to your word.
I seek you with all my heart;
do not let me stray from your commands.
I have hidden your word in my heart
that I might not sin against you.

I KEPT ASKING MYSELF, "WHAT
could possibly be so interesting about that tattered old book? Why
would this frail old woman get up every morning at 5:30 and read it?
And when she finally finished reading through this massive volume,

why did she go right back to the first page and start reading it all over again?"

These were some of the questions I pondered when I was ten years old. The frail old woman was my paternal grandmother, who lived with us on our farm. And the tattered old book was an ancient German Bible, written in a gothic script that was completely indecipherable to me. There were no pictures in that old Bible, yet this mysterious book continually held my grandmother's interest. What secrets did those pages contain?

One day I asked her, "Grandma, how many times have you read through that old Bible?"

"Thirteen times," she said with a smile, and then she added, "I'm on to the fourteenth time now. I hope to finish it again before I die."

Grandma talked about dying quite often. She addressed the topic with an enthusiasm that I found quite disturbing. She looked forward to leaving this world for what she said was a far better place. I thought she was a bit selfish in this regard. She didn't seem to care about how sad we would feel about her departure.

She was a curious old woman, or so I thought. But she was always more than kind in everything she said and did, and I loved her dearly. Maybe that tattered old book had some influence on her personality and the warm, affirmative life she lived before us all.

At age ten, it was pure curiosity that sent me on a grand quest to discover what was written in that ancient book. Without prompting from anyone, I began reading the Bible. Actually, it wasn't Grandma's German Bible that I read, but rather an enormous King James family Bible which my parent's had recently purchased.

Yes, there were some indecipherable parts, but I soon mastered the *thee's* and *thou's*. After a bit of mental gymnastics I was able to use *hath*, *doth* and *saith* right along with the seventeenth-century translators.

Though it was curiosity that brought me to the Bible, it was the Holy Spirit who brought the Bible to life. I quickly cruised through all four Gospels. I picked up speed as, with wide-eyed interest, I read the Book of Acts. Then I tackled the Epistles and the Book of Revelation head on. In a relatively short time I read all of the New Testament. Instead of watching television, I was devouring the Bible. After doing my family chores and homework, I would head straight for that huge family Bible. The Old Testament was next on my list and, one by one, the books of the Pentateuch went into my mental hopper. Next I churned through the Old Testament historical books. Job, Psalms, Proverbs, and Ecclesiastes were a bit tough on the circuits in my literary processor, but I conquered them. Finally I reached the major and minor prophets; I read them all.

At age ten, in the space of about four months, I read the entire Bible. It was a remarkable feat—one that I have repeated several times over the years—but never again have I done it in such a short time. There was a divine hunger inside me for God's Word. It was hunger stoked by curiosity and fanned by the wind of the Holy Spirit.

"How can a young man keep his way pure?"

When I reached my teen years, this question rose up to haunt me. Suddenly a whole new set of temptations came slithering down the path of life. Many of those temptations were very attractive. The psalmist's question came echoing across the ages. It is a question that is as relevant now as when it was penned almost three thousand years ago. Is it possible for a young man to live a pure life? The psalmist's question reminds me of Jeremiah's question, *"can a leopard remove its spots?"* (Jeremiah 13:23 CEV).

The simple, straightforward answer to both questions is, no. Leopards by their very nature are spotted. Young men by their very nature are sinful, sex-obsessed and brimful of testosterone-drenched bravado. Young men and purity do not easily fit in the same sentence. They clash like lions among lambs—like lacy pink frills on a boar in a mud wallow.

197

"How can a young man keep his way pure?" Why attempt the impossible? Why even set such a goal? Why try to reverse the course of human nature? The human soul is a sin-spotted soul. Can this manly leopard remove his spots?

Why would a young man want to keep his way pure? Why not chase every pretty skirt in town? Why not have some fun? Why not eat, drink, and be merry? We only pass through this life once. Why not live it up?

But if the God of the universe has called men into relationship with Him, then purity and holiness are at the very core of that relationship. If we are called to be with God—to dwell in harmony with Him—then we must embrace holiness. To embrace God is to embrace holiness. Those sin spots have got to go. If we are to walk with God, we must willingly walk away from soul-fouling sin.

Why would a young man want to keep his way pure? So he can walk with God. So he can hear His voice. So he can know the love of the Father. That's part of the reason. If we fix our eyes on the One who calls us to walk out of our sin-spotted skin, then there is hope for the way. There is a reward for those who take up the purity challenge. As my grandma knew so very well, the pure way—the way of holiness—has its rewards in both this life and the next.

The writer of the Book of Hebrews urges on the young faith runners with these words:

> *Let us throw off everything that hinders and the sin that so easily entangles, and let us run with perseverance the race marked out for us. Let us fix our eyes on Jesus, the author and perfecter of our faith, who for the joy set before him endured the cross, scorning its shame, and sat down at the right hand of the throne of God (Hebrews 12:1–2).*

Young men need to fix their eyes. Young men have wandering eyes. Purity requires fixed eyes—eyes that are fixed solely on Jesus.

In a world awash in pornography, we all need fixed eyes—eyes fixed on Jesus—eyes that see the cross—eyes that see the blood-drenched cross. Purity comes at a price. It cost the heavenly Father the life of His very own Son.

A young man named Jesus—in flesh like my own, in skin like my own—poured out His life's blood to make me pure.

Fix your eyes on Him!

There is a spot remover. It's called the blood of Christ. At the foot of the cross this manly leopard can remove his spots. Jesus can make me pure; He can make you pure.

"How can a young man keep his way pure? By living according to your word."

After this blood-based spot remover has been applied, there is still a life to live. Now with your sins forgiven, with your sin spots removed, live according to God's Word. Pray for God's Word to come alive and walk off the pages of your Bible. Make the following words your confession and your prayer:

"I seek you with all my heart; do not let me stray from your commands."

You may ask, "How do I go about seeking God with all my heart?"

You simply start by looking for God. Watch for Him. He is at work in your life. He will not abandon the one He redeemed at the cost of His own dear Son. He's not a deadbeat dad. This heavenly Father cares about the sons and daughters He has brought into this new life. Watch daily for His guiding hand. He is not far away. The LORD has given us His promise on that. *"The LORD is near to all who call on him, to all who call on him in truth"* (Psalm 145:18).

God arranges your circumstances. Whatever your age, you are His young man or woman now. Expect to meet Him around the next corner, and He will show up. When you need Him most, God is there. When you least expect Him, the LORD will take you by surprise. You are His son or daughter now, and His presence in your life is more certain than the next sunrise.

Obedience to God's commands does not always come easily. Our old nature rebels. Ask for the LORD's help. Speak out your prayer, "*Do not let me stray from your commands.*"

If you seek after God, soon this will become your faith profession: "*I have hidden your word in my heart that I might not sin against you.*"

Now this is one of the deepest secrets to be found in my grandma's tattered old book. Hiding God's Word is a rather curious metaphor. How do I hide God's Word in my heart? The answers may seem obvious. Hear it. Read it. Study it. Meditate on it. Apply it to life. Commit it to memory.

All of these methods will get God's Word into my heart. Right? Wrong.

Simply hearing God's Word will not get it into your heart. Hell is filled with hearers of God's Word. Perhaps you don't believe me? Let's check in on Jesus' teaching regarding this topic. Jesus' story of the rich man and Lazarus, the beggar, is a perfect illustration of this point. See Luke 16:19–31. The rich man and his brothers were regular hearers of the Word of God, but it made no difference to the eternal destiny of their souls. The Word of God lay lifeless on the surface of their hearts.

Jesus' parable of the sower and the seed (Matthew 13:1–23) sheds some real light on this metaphor of hiding God's Word in our heart. Hearing is a shallow experience. All too often, the heard word has no depth. To get depth we need understanding. Most often understanding springs out of application, not out of hearing. I can hear a particular truth a thousand times but it isn't really mine until I apply it to my own life. Applied truth bears fruit. It yields results. The applied truth of God's Word is self-validating. It has the life of the Spirit within it. Only when we apply the Word are we living according to it.

But heard truth lies on the surface—a tasty morsel ready for the devil to snatch away. The heard Word has all the potential of the applied Word but none of the yield, because it has not penetrated the heart.

We need to become pregnant with God's Word. Pregnancy is never achieved through the ear. Young men need a deeper experience. We all need hearts that are warmed by the love of God and wide open to His holy Word—His seed—His eternal, life-producing Word.

Yes, hide God's Word in your heart. Hear God's holy Word. Read it. Study it. Meditate on it. Commit it to memory. Above all, apply it to your life that you might not sin against Him! In that way the written Word will be transformed into Spirit-born words that will live in your heart.

This is, after all, all about Him. This is all about being close to Him! This is about loving *"the* LORD *your God with all your heart and with all your soul and with all your mind"* (Matthew 22:37).

You have not come to a truth. You have come to the Truth, the Life, and the Way. You have come to Christ, the spotless One—the One whose way is pure. You have not come to just a tattered book. You have come to the Word that became flesh and dwelt among us. This living Word *"was with God in the beginning. Through him all things were made; without him nothing was made that has been made. In him was life, and that life was the light of men"* (John 1:2–4).

His life was the light of men—of young men and even ten-year-old boys.

Oh yes, and grandmas too.

Bringing Life to the Psalms

1. What are you doing to hide God's Word in your heart? What routines have you established that bring you into daily contact with God's Word?

2. Preaching is most often the focal point of any church service. It is a format that produces hearers of the Word, but does it produce disciples? Jesus commanded us to make disciples, not merely hearers of the Word. What can you or your church do to help facilitate the heart-changing application of God's Word?

3. What special challenges do young men face as they try to live a pure life? Have you personally taken up the purity challenge? Jesus worked with young men whose faith grew as they lived with Him in fellowship. These men changed the world. Are you part of a network of men who are in heart-opening fellowship with Christ?

4. Take a moment to read Jesus' story of the rich man and Lazarus as found in Luke 16:19–31. What application may this account have on how you hear God's Word?

5. "The applied truth of God's Word is self-validating." What does that statement mean? Have you experienced an instance when God's Word proved itself true when you applied it to your particular life circumstance?

I Will Not
Neglect Your Word

Praise be to you, O LORD;
teach me your decrees.
With my lips I recount
all the laws that come from your mouth.
I rejoice in following your statutes
as one rejoices in great riches.
I meditate on your precepts
and consider your ways.
I delight in your decrees;
I will not neglect your word.

PSALM 119 IS THE LONGEST
psalm in the Bible. It is also an acrostic poem, which in this case,
means each stanza of this poetic psalm begins with a different letter
of the Hebrew alphabet. The section above, for instance, begins with

the letter Beth, which roughly corresponds to our letter B. Also, within each alphabetic stanza are eight verses, all of which begin with the same Hebrew letter. In this way, the psalm's composer works his way through the entire twenty-two letters of the Hebrew alphabet. This psalm is in fact a remarkable literary composition which was originally structured to be memorized like the alphabet. Unfortunately for the English reader, much of the elaborate, intricate beauty of this psalm is lost the moment it is translated from its original language.

The theme of this psalm is consistent throughout. It is a poetic testimony in praise of God's holy, unchanging Word. Here we find the alpha and omega of the psalms—a literary tribute to the A to Z wonder of God's Word. Every letter trumpets the salutary goodness of God's written Word. Charles Spurgeon, the nineteenth century theologian, has called Psalm 119, "a pearl island, or better still, a garden of sweet flowers."[6]

In this psalm, we find these immortal words of comfort and encouragement: "*Your word is a lamp to my feet and a light for my path*" (Psalm 119:105).

Throughout the ages, the saints of God have found that light for the journey comes streaming through the written pages of the Word of God. Where can we turn in times of despair? How can we scale mountains of fear? How can we cross an ocean of worry? In this sin-darkened world, the Word of God stands secure. It sends out a beam of radiant truth to light the traveler's path. Is it any wonder then, that the psalmist declares, "*I have put my hope in your word*" (Psalm 119:147)?

While Psalm 119 shouts out the eternal praises of God's Word, it does so from a kneeling position. There is an unmistakable

---

[6] *The Treasury of David, Psalms 111-150* (Classic Reflections on the Wisdom of the Psalms, Volume 3) by Charles H. Spurgeon, Hendrickson Publishing, 2005

posture to this psalm. It rings most true when it is spoken by a worshipper on his knees. This is a psalm filled with humble supplication. It is humble supplication that kneels and bows low before the Holy One of Israel.

There is an earnest pleading in this psalm that springs from the realization that, apart from God and His Holy Word, personal holiness and salvation are impossible. Hence, we have the opening question that frames this stanza, "*How can a young man keep his way pure?*"

But in His mercy the LORD has provided a response:"*Praise be to you, O LORD; teach me your decrees.*"

Unless God teaches me His decrees, I stumble through life lost, without direction, meaning, or purpose. In reality, the "eat, drink, and be merry" philosophy that governs the actions of so many in this world simply springs naturally from their lost state. Hedonism is, after all, a rather logical response if life has no meaning or purpose, or if our souls have no eternal destiny.

But to the soul who has heard God's whisper in the wind or caught a glimpse of His unfading glory in the setting sun, hedonism has lost much of its allure. The soul that takes the long view—that sees beyond the grave—lives life in a different light. We are called to live on a higher plane—a plane that is sustained and nourished by God's life-giving, life-invigorating Word.

So in humility with the psalmist, we cry out to the LORD, "*Teach me your decrees.*"

Now, aware of our fallen position—from a position of need—we cry out again to the LORD, "*Teach me your decrees.*"

The arrogant and self-satisfied are unfamiliar with this prayer. It has no resonance within them. This is the prayer of the hungry and the thirsty. It is Jesus, the Word Incarnate, who takes it upon Himself to personally answer this prayer. Through the Beatitudes He answers the cry of our heart, "*Blessed are those who hunger and thirst for righteousness, for they will be filled*" (Matthew 5:6).

There is a righteousness that does not spring from our performance or our merit. It does not come from observing the law. It comes directly from the crucified and risen Christ, the One who knew no sin. This righteousness—the righteousness of Christ—is credited to our account by faith. As the apostle Paul asserts, *"we have believed in Jesus Christ, that we might be justified by faith in Christ and not by the works of the law; for by the works of the law no flesh shall be justified"* (Galatians 2:16 NKJV).

Did the writer of Psalm 119 understand the true source of holiness, or was he simply trying to achieve holiness through his own human effort? Is the psalmist's focus on the law of the LORD and His commands and decrees just a misdirected reflection of legalistic Old Testament thinking? For today's believers who look back in history from this side of the cross, this is a valid question.

On this point, the psalmist's prayer later in Psalm 119 is truly insightful. Notice both his choice of words and his posture in supplication, *"May your unfailing love come to me, O LORD, your salvation according to your promise; then I will answer the one who taunts me, for I trust in your word"* (Psalm 119:41).

Clearly the psalmist saw his need for salvation—salvation that comes freely from a God of grace and unfailing love. Secondly, in the same way as New Testament believers find salvation, the psalmist puts his trust in the Word of God and the LORD's sure promises—promises that include the coming of a Savior-Redeemer. Satan's taunts are no match for the believer who has put his faith in the LORD and His Word.

Biblical revelation is progressive through time. The full revelation of God's way of redemption was not revealed to the Old Testament prophets. They saw in part and prophesied in part concerning the coming of our Lord and Savior, Jesus Christ. But the partial nature of their revelation does not invalidate their testimony or the authority of their words. Even as the above passage reveals, they saw the way of salvation with an uncanny accuracy—an accuracy that was Holy Spirit breathed.

In fact, the apostle Peter validates the ministry of the Old Testament writers by declaring of these men that they *"spoke from God as they were carried along by the Holy Spirit"* (2 Peter 1:21).

Again Peter confirms the authority of the Old Testament Scriptures by quoting the words of Isaiah: *"All men are like grass, and all their glory is like the flowers of the field; the grass withers and the flowers fall, but the word of the Lord stands forever"* (1 Peter 1:24–25).

If the Word of the LORD stands forever, why do so many Christians discount the Old Testament Scriptures? They may be Scriptures, but we discount them. They have been dumped into the half-off bin at the back of our scriptural storehouse. Actually, they're in the front of the Bible, but for many of us, they are in that unused, unread portion. Mentally, we have moved them to the back forty. They have become the back forty-four—out of sight and out of mind.

But the words of Psalm 119 break into our mind. Here we have some radical thinking—a radical all-out devotion to God's Word.

"With my lips I recount all the laws that come from your mouth. I rejoice in following your statutes as one rejoices in great riches."

In my mind, recounting something with my lips sounds a lot like a rehearsal. Have you rehearsed God's laws? Doing a rehearsal with my lips sounds a lot like recitation. Have you recited God's laws? And how can anyone recite something without memorizing it? Have you committed portions of God's Word to memory?

Memorization is a skill that has fallen by the wayside. At one time, it was routinely taught and practiced in our schools. Alas, in many classes and in many schools, those days are long gone. For many years, the church was the last bastion of memorization. But in many churches too this skill has fallen by the wayside. As a result, God's Word has fallen by the wayside.

In recent years, the birds of the air have had plenty to devour because God's people have forgotten how to hide the Word of the LORD in their hearts. But Satan's emissaries have been busy doing double duty. Not only have they been snatching away the Word of God, they also have been filling the empty spots in our minds. They have been planting illicit images where God's Word should be growing.

Is it any wonder then that the church is anemic? The Spirit-infused bread of life has not been digested and incorporated into the church, the earthbound *corpus Christi*.

Memorization is hard work; it takes discipline. A disciple embraces discipline. Are you a disciple in the body of Christ? Then you will discover there is a joy that comes through incorporating God's Word more fully into your mind and into your life.

The psalmist found a wellspring of joy in the Word of God. Hear his words: *"I rejoice in following your statutes as one rejoices in great riches."*

Memorization very naturally leads to incorporation. The Word becomes part of us, just as the food we eat. God's Word is lived out, expressed daily through our lives. We follow the written Word—the statutes—and in so doing we are following Christ. After all, it was Jesus who told His disciples, *"If you love me, you will obey what I command"* (John 14:15).

When we obey, the Word becomes fully alive in us. As it was at Christ's conception, once again the Word becomes incarnate. But this time, God's Word is alive in us—alive in our earthen vessels.

Are you rich in God's Word? Are you finding joy in following Jesus' commands? If you are discovering that joy, a wonderful promise awaits you. Jesus said, *"If anyone loves me, he will obey my teaching. My Father will love him, and we will come to him and make our home with him"* (John 14:23).

The empty spot in the garden of our heart will be filled. Jesus will live there through the power of His Word. Your heart will become His dwelling place.

Meditating on God's Word makes room for Jesus in our mind. The psalmist knew not only the secret of a clean mind, he also knew how to keep his mind occupied, healthy, and active. Hear him again: *"I meditate on your precepts and consider your ways."*

Unlike mind-emptying transcendental meditation, biblical meditation fills the mind with God's holy Word. Our mind becomes a garden of life—a garden of sweet flowers—bringing glory to God our Creator.

By meditating on God's Word and His ways, we put into practice the apostle Paul's advice to us: *"whatever is true, whatever is noble, whatever is right, whatever is pure, whatever is lovely, whatever is admirable—if anything is excellent or praiseworthy—think about such things"* (Philippians 4:8).

As we meditate on these things and put them into practice, the God of all peace will be with us. He resides in His Word. His presence in us will manifest itself through an ever-increasing measure of spiritual power when we open our hearts and our minds to meditate on His Word. Then we will find joy coming to us through God's Word. The psalmist's confession will become our own. *"I delight in your decrees."*

"I will not neglect your word."

For me, these words have become a daily challenge and a personal commitment. I will not neglect God's Word. When I am walking in His garden, Jesus finds me there.

Bringing Life to the Psalms

1. Memorization and meditation are sisters. Both practices bury God's Word more deeply in our minds. The buried seed of God's Word germinates, grows, and bears fruit. Commit yourself now to

memorize God's Word. Psalm 119 *Beth* is a wonderful place to begin this life-changing practice.

2. When the Word of God takes root in our hearts, we become living epistles—letters from God to a lost generation. You are the only Bible many in this world will ever read. Take a moment to read 2 Corinthians 3:1–3. What do those around you see when they read your life?

3. Is the Old Testament in your scriptural deep-discount bin? What relevance does it have for your life today? Have there been instances when an Old Testament passage or story significantly impacted your life? What steps can be taken to honor the whole of God's Word more fully in our churches today?

4. Take time to read all of Psalm 119. Highlight those verses that particularly speak to your heart. Review those same passages later in the day or the week. Take time to think on these things. By doing so, you are meditating on God's Word.

5. Does a Bible verse prompt you to action? Do it. God will be with you to fulfill His Word.

6. Reread Psalm 119 *Beth*. What is God saying to you through this psalm?

I Lift Up my Eyes

A Song of Ascents

I lift up my eyes to the hills—
where does my help come from?
My help comes from the LORD,
the Maker of heaven and earth.
He will not let your foot slip—
he who watches over you will not slumber;
indeed, he who watches over Israel
will neither slumber nor sleep.
The LORD *watches over you—*
the LORD *is your shade at your right hand;*
the sun will not harm you by day,
nor the moon by night.
The LORD *will keep you from all harm—*
he will watch over your life;
the LORD *will watch over your coming and going*
both now and forevermore.

PSALM 121 IS A SONG OF
Ascents, and as such it was a psalm intended for use by pilgrims as
they journeyed to Jerusalem. This particular psalm was most often
sung or chanted as the pilgrims set out from Jericho. As they lifted up

their eyes, the sharply rising hill country of Judah stretched off into the distance. Hill after hill rose up before them.

This final portion of the pilgrimage was truly an ascent. From the Dead Sea plain, the road to Jerusalem climbs nearly five thousand feet (fifteen hundred meters). This is truly an ascent—an ascent from the Dead Sea, the lowest point on earth's surface, to the heights of Mount Zion.

For the bone-weary pilgrims who had already walked more than sixty miles(one hundred kilometers) from Galilee, the sight of those distant hills must have brought a measure of aching discouragement. Here was a looming challenge. Could they make the final ascent? The opening question of this psalm was not a matter of poetic whimsy. It was spoken in earnest.

"I lift up my eyes to the hills—where does my help come from?"

The weary pilgrim may well be asking, "Having come this far, can I complete this journey? Do I have enough energy—enough stamina— to climb those hills? Will I be able to reach Zion? I am exhausted now before I even start the ascent. I can't do this on my own."

"Where does my help come from?"

The psalmist's answer resounds off those ancient hills. Even today, it echoes down through the ages and reverberates through the chambers of the heart.

"My help comes from the LORD, the Maker of heaven and earth."

I cannot make it on my own. Realistically, I am incapable of this final climb. Zion is unreachable in my own strength. But all things are possible with God. He is the Maker of heaven and earth. Surely the Maker of the earth can help me move across this tiny portion of the planet that He has formed. He is my help. *"My help comes from the LORD!"*

This bold profession from the psalmist reflects reality for all who have answered our Savior's call to walk in faith. We start from the lowest point. Jesus does not call us from the heights. He calls us from the Dead Sea—a place of both physical and spiritual death. Paul, the apostle, makes this perfectly clear.

> *As for you, you were dead in your transgressions and sins, in which you used to live when you followed the ways of this world and the ruler of the kingdom of the air, the spirit that is now at work in those who are disobedient. All of us also lived among them at one time, gratifying the cravings of our sinful nature and following its desires and thoughts* (Ephesians 2:1–2).

It is from this low point that we lift up our eyes. If we look at ourselves—at our sin-steeped past—there is no hope. It is just as St. Paul says: we are dead in our transgressions and sins. If we lift up our eyes to the road ahead—to the upward-sloping road of righteousness—we will become discouraged. All we see are hills—obstacles—as far as the eye can see. Holiness is not an innate human response. The way is hard; the climb is steep, even impossible. There is no hope there. No, we must lift our eyes higher yet. We must look past the hills to the LORD, the Maker of heaven and earth.

"*Where does my help come from? My help comes from the LORD, the Maker of heaven and earth.*"

How high are you lifting your eyes? If we look to the LORD, there is hope. Through Him, the way becomes possible. In Him there is grace for the journey. Through His love and mercy we are no longer spiritually dead. We have a new life—a new life in Christ. The road ahead has, in fact, been prepared for us. It is as Paul asserts, "*But because of his great love for us, God, who is rich in mercy, made us alive with Christ even when we were dead in transgressions—it is by grace you have been saved*" (Ephesians 2:4–5).

Having been born again through faith, it is Christ who now walks with us on this earthly pilgrimage. We can leave behind the

Dead Sea region with all its life-draining futility. We can leave behind the fetid sea of sin. We are not traveling alone now. Our forerunner, our brother, the King, is walking with us.

He is walking beside me. When I lift up my eyes, He comes into view.

As I walk on, His words are my constant comfort and encouragement. Jesus speaks to the pilgrim, *"I am the light of the world. Whoever follows me will never walk in darkness, but will have the light of life"* (John 8:12).

Here in this psalm we have our LORD's sure promise.

"He will not let your foot slip—he who watches over you will not slumber; indeed, he who watches over Israel will neither slumber nor sleep."

For the weary Jewish pilgrim, a foot slip was no small mishap. If a foot slipped and an ankle twisted, the journey was over. There was no point in proceeding. Why add more agonizing miles to the journey? Why inconvenience others with your injury? The pilgrim would find a safe place to rest and recover, perhaps at an inn, while the others in his party would proceed to Zion.

The Christian pilgrim's constant prayer should be, "Do not let my foot slip. Let my step be firm; let my path be straight."

This is why our Lord taught us to pray, *"Lead us not into temptation, but deliver us from the evil one"* (Matthew 6:13).

The LORD is always alert to that prayer. It is His prayer and it is His desire to answer it. We can rest assured that He will watch over us. We can rest—yes, truly rest. We can put our minds at ease because He will not. He will not rest. He will not slumber or sleep. Like a mother keeps vigil over a desperately sick child, so the LORD watches over every move we make—every time we stir—so constant is His care.

Those who are saved by grace can find rest in His grace. *"He will not let your foot slip."* His goal is your goal. He longs to welcome you to Zion, to the House of God, to your eternal home.

So it then follows that *"the LORD watches over you—the LORD is your shade at your right hand; the sun will not harm you by day, nor the moon by night."*

Interestingly, Jesus told one of his best-known parables about this particular journey—the journey from Jerusalem down to Jericho. In truth, it is the pilgrim's journey of Psalm 121 done in reverse. We know it as the parable of the Good Samaritan (Luke 10:25–37). From this parable we discover that the descent from Jerusalem to Jericho was not only steep and treacherous, it was also fraught with danger. The steep hills, rills, and canyons were ideal hideouts for highway robbers. They could pounce on the unsuspecting traveler from behind any one of ten thousand rocks. One never knew what danger might lurk around the next sharp curve in the road. Ambushes on this route were common. It was wise to travel in a group. The lone traveler was an easy target for marauding thieves.

When we decide to follow Christ, we instantly become a target for Satan's attack. He and his demonic minions lie in wait for the unsuspecting faith pilgrim. The lone believer can quickly become the wounded-and-dying believer. The struggling believer may soon become the fallen believer—fallen and half-dead.

We are our brothers' keepers. There is safety in numbers. We are to journey together. So with this in mind,

> *Let us hold unswervingly to the hope we profess, for he who promised is faithful. And let us consider how we may spur one another on toward love and good deeds. Let us not give up meeting together, as some are in the habit of doing, but let us encourage one another—and all the more as you see the Day approaching* (Hebrews 10:23–25).

In addition, we need the LORD's protective shield round about us. We need His promise. *"The LORD is your shade at your right hand; the sun will not harm you by day, nor the moon by night."*

Pray for the LORD's round-the-clock protection. Put on the full armor of God. The LORD's pilgrim is also the LORD's warrior against spiritual forces of darkness. The apostle Paul reminds us to *"take up the shield of faith, with which you can extinguish all the flaming arrows of the evil one. Take the helmet of salvation and the sword of the Spirit, which is the word of God. And pray in the Spirit on all occasions with all kinds of prayers and requests. With this in mind, be alert and always keep on praying for all the saints"* (Ephesians 6:16–18).

As you do all these things on your upward journey, *"the LORD will keep you from all harm—He will watch over your life; the LORD will watch over your coming and going both now and forevermore."*

It is amazing how much distance you can cover on foot when your pace is steady and when you make a straight path, or a direct line, to your objective. I was reminded of this truth just this afternoon. Once again I am back in Chicago for some drama events. Once again I went for a walk along scenic Lincoln Park on the shore of Lake Michigan. But unlike my leisurely stroll of last summer, today from the outset, I set a pace—a brisk pace—and I had an objective in mind.

My objective was a lighthouse at the end of a concrete pier that juts out into the aquamarine waters of the lake. Having set my sights on this lighthouse, I made a beeline for it. For me, taking the most direct route sometimes meant stepping off of the well-worn path and heading off across country.

Following Christ is like that. If we have Him in our sights, the well-worn path that others follow may not be for us. Those other paths take us to other destinations. They may even take us close to the Lighthouse, but not to the Lighthouse.

When you lift up your eyes, lift them to the One you are following. Lift them to Jesus. Then let your feet follow the most direct path to Him, regardless of where others are walking. If your pace is steady and unwavering, and if your course is straight, the miles will fly by.

The distance flew by for me. I reached my objective, the lighthouse, so quickly that I set another objective. There was another lighthouse still farther up the shore. I maintained my pace and again I took the most direct route. Again I was surprise by the speed at which I covered the distance. When I reached this second objective, a whole new vista opened up. New opportunities presented themselves.

If you fix your eyes on Christ, He will bring you to the summit of the next hill. A new adventure—a new vista—awaits.

When I look back over the years of my faith pilgrimage, I can see that my progress has not always been steady or direct. There have been distractions. My pace has been erratic. Other paths—well-worn paths—have intersected with the direct path to Christ. At times I have drifted down those intersecting paths.

But then I lift up my eyes. I lift my eyes to the hill—the hill of my salvation. There is a cross on that hill. Though Jesus' hands are pinned, He beckons me closer. I fix my eyes on Him. He draws me up—up the round stone hill of Calvary.

> *Let us throw off everything that hinders and the sin that so easily entangles, and let us run with perseverance the race marked out for us. Let us fix our eyes on Jesus, the author and perfecter of our faith, who for the joy set before him endured the cross, scorning its shame, and sat down at the right hand of the throne of God (Hebrews 12:1–2).*

"Jesus, draw me to the summit. I fix my eyes on You."
A new vista awaits.

Bringing Life to the Psalms

1. In our urban environment, we live in an artificial world—a world planned for the automobile. It seems many of us have forgotten why the LORD gave us legs, yet we talk about our walk of faith. This week, plan a walk. Be sure to take Jesus with you. Ask Him to speak to you on the way. Remember: the resurrected Christ joined His disciples as they walked to Emmaus.

2. Have you ever been distracted from the path? Was it immediately obvious that you had left the path God had called you to walk? What brought you back? Did a particular event trigger your return?

3. In a world of flashing distractions, how do we keep our eyes fixed on Jesus? In your walk of faith, when your pace is steady and progress is readily apparent, what sort of things are you doing?

4. Are you your brother's or sister's keeper? Have you helped someone recently in their faith walk? Have you needed help? Open, honest communication is essential. Satan attacks and silences believers, but our Father invites us to speak to Him and to each other.

5. Reread Psalm 121. What is God saying to you by His Spirit?

Filled With Laughter

A Song of ascents.

When the LORD brought back the captives to Zion,
we were like men who dreamed.
Our mouths were filled with laughter,
our tongues with songs of joy.
Then it was said among the nations,
"The LORD has done great things for them."
The LORD has done great things for us,
and we are filled with joy.

Restore our fortunes, O LORD,
like streams in the Negev.
Those who sow in tears
will reap with songs of joy.
He who goes out weeping,
carrying seed to sow,
will return with songs of joy,
carrying sheaves with him.

I CANNOT READ THIS PSALM—
Psalm 126—without immediately identifying with it. I have lived
this psalm. I have experienced the reality of it.

That is a rather bold statement; some might call it an ignorant or arrogant statement. The historical context of this psalm is readily identifiable. The psalmist is commenting on the joyous return of the exiles following the seventy-year Babylonian captivity—an event that occurred in the sixth century before the birth of Christ. How could anyone alive today claim that they have lived or experienced this particular psalm? None of us were present during these dramatic events in Jewish history.

But again I repeat: I have lived this psalm; I have experienced the reality of it.

The whole premise of this book is built on the notion that the psalms can come alive within us. The writer of the book of Hebrews reminds us that *"the word of God is living and active"* (Hebrews 4:12).

What is there, then, to prevent this living Word from coming alive within us? Why can we not experience this active Word of God transforming and transporting us to the throne of grace? Only two things hinder us from living in the power and wonder of the Word of God. They are sin and unbelief. Sin and unbelief are only too eager to form within us a constricting bond that smothers the Spirit-empowered Word.

But when the power of sin is broken and unbelief is purged from the doubting soul—oh, what liberty awaits! The Word of God comes alive within us. The LORD is then free to do great and glorious things in us and through us.

That was my experience as a young man in the early 1970s. The LORD was bringing back the captives to Zion, *"and we were like men who dreamed. Our mouths were filled with laughter, our tongues with songs of joy."*

I was caught up in the vortex of the Jesus People movement of that time, and amazing things were happening. Young men and women were coming to faith in Christ at a phenomenal rate. At every church meeting, newcomers were finding the forgiveness they needed. The prodigals were coming home in droves. Every gathering closed with a baptismal service as new believers affirmed their faith in the crucified and risen Christ. There was a heady, infectious joy in the church that could not be contained.

At that time, "*Our mouths were filled with laughter, our tongues with songs of joy.*"

The spontaneity of the worship experience during those days was truly astonishing. New songs were born—born by the Spirit—right within the corporate worship time. Many of them came directly from the Scriptures. The Psalms became the source book for our worship. The captives—captives of sin and Satan—had been set free, and now there was a new song in our hearts and on our lips—a song of praise to our God. We could not keep this to ourselves. Who could possibly contain the overflowing goodness and mercy of God?

This ingathering of souls was God's doing. A lost generation was arrested by the Almighty. He was turning us around and we were discovering Jesus. And this move of the Holy Spirit did not begin in the church. No, it began in the flophouses and hippie communes. It started on the street—in the world—the sin-saturated world. It did not start with saintly scholars and philosophers, but rather with the young and restless, the hitchhikers and misfits. God was calling them to Himself, and He was miraculously transforming lives as only can God do.

Because this new thing that God was doing started in the world, many Christians were suspicious of it. Could this really be God? Many churches stood aloof. But those who welcomed these misfits found themselves overwhelmed and transformed by what God was doing. He had initiated this and He stood at the center of it.

Soon the Jesus movement was affecting the entire youth culture. "Amazing Grace" became the number one hit on top-forty radio. A half-dozen hit songs spoke of the Man from Galilee. *Time* magazine ran a cover story on how the youth across the continent were discovering Jesus. Suddenly, it was *cool* to love Jesus and to follow Him.

I was a frontline witness to all this. I was seeing lives changed all around me. Close friends who were far from God were suddenly having life-altering encounters with Jesus. *"We were like men who dreamed."* And in that dream Jesus had come to live among us. His long flowing hair had become our own. He was with us again, just as He had been with that band of fishermen on the Sea of Galilee and the nets were full with fish—boat-swamping full with fish.

"Our mouths were filled with laughter, our tongues with songs of joy. Then it was said among the nations, 'The LORD has done great things for them.'"

The world knows when God is doing something remarkable, and the psalmist records the ancient world heard that the captive Jewish nation had been released. The exiles were free to return to their homeland, and return they did. In the early 1970s, the modern world heard that Jesus was bringing young people to Himself. They too were free—set free from a load of guilt and sin, set free from addictions and hang ups—free to love and serve God with hearts washed pure by the blood of the Lamb.

"The LORD has done great things for us, and we are filled with joy!"

That was my experience—an experience that was shared by thousands of others across this continent during that remarkable time. It was the LORD's doing. He did great things for us—things I will never forget.

But ...

But there is a pause in this psalm. This is a psalm written in two distinct sections or stanzas. In most translations, this break between stanzas is indicated by a blank line. The psalmist abruptly transitions from joyous triumph to sober petition, from exuberance to sobbing desperation. We are left wondering what happened in between. What happened in that blank line? Why this sharp transition? In bleak desolation the psalmist pleads, *"Restore our fortunes, O LORD, like streams in the Negev."*

Streams in the Negev are intermittent. A raging torrent one day becomes a mere trickle the next day and then nothing on the third day. The boisterous river of joy turns into a blank line on the desert floor. Nothing—just nothing.

The Negev is the parched desert region to the south of the land of Judah. Cloud bursts there can produce streams in the barren desert, and with the sudden arrival of this moisture, long dormant seeds spring to life. Suddenly new life abounds. But without further moisture, the scorching sun takes its toll. The harsh environment reasserts its dominance. Land that was briefly lush and verdant reverts to desert dust.

Is it any wonder then that the psalmist cries out, *"Restore our fortunes, O LORD, like streams in the Negev."* The psalmist longs for the flow of new life to continue.

And right along with the psalmist I cry, "Send your river flowing through here once again. Send a cloudburst of your mercy down on this nation again. Invade this culture again. Turn our young people to Jesus yet again. Touch this new generation. Let them find themselves walking with You, the living Christ. You did it once, Lord, and I saw it. I experienced it. Now do it again! Do it again, not for me, but for those who don't know You. Do great things for them. Set them free from the sin and the lies that ensnare them. Touch all of us once again!"

"Restore our fortunes, O LORD, like streams in the Negev."

In those days of the 1970s, at the height of what God was doing, I saw a dozen young men line up in the freezing cold. They had arrived early. They were waiting for the pastor to arrive on a Saturday night to unlock the church so they could come in and give their hearts to Jesus. I saw hundreds of young people being baptized at that same church—more than three hundred in a year, one for every day of the year. God was adding to the church *"daily those who were being saved"* (Acts 2:47).

This was not about the Holy Spirit tickling the church's funny bone. It was about sinners finding God. Time after time I saw the lost crowding the altar at the close of the service. They wanted Jesus—nothing more, nothing less—just Jesus.

Now only the faithful come to the altar, if anyone comes at all.

"Restore our fortunes, O LORD."

I echo the psalmist's prayer, *"Restore our fortunes, O LORD."*

Fortunately, we are provided with the promise of God's Word in tandem with the psalmist's petition, *"Those who sow in tears will reap with songs of joy."*

If you live in a dry land, water it with your tears. If the wind of God's Spirit is a distant memory, remember that seasons change. The seed of God's Word is still viable. It is always power-packed and ready to spring to life. Just add water.

"He who goes out weeping, carrying seed to sow, will return with songs of joy, carrying sheaves with him."

God's promise stands sure and certain but, for us, two questions remain. Are you going out weeping? Are you carrying seed to sow?

Perhaps the church in Canada has never experienced a harsher spiritual climate than that which exists today. We live in a society that by and large has turned its back on God. The gospel message is often treated with contempt or outright ridicule. The church exists in a spiritual desert. Figuratively, Canada is the Negev.

In such a harsh climate, the natural inclination is to cocoon ourselves away. The world out there is inhospitable. It's best to stay inside, to huddle amongst ourselves. Isn't it better to cloister ourselves away than to expose ourselves to the harsh elements and the criticism of others? Let's circle the wagons and entertain ourselves. This has become the unspoken *modus operandi* for many churches.

Into our cloistered existence the psalmist speaks. He instructs us to step out of our sheltered place. He tells us to go out weeping. What a bizarre command! Weeping is for private places. Why would we want to go out into the world weeping? Yet, this is what we are encouraged to do. Could it be that we are to get out of our churches and cry? Cry over what?

How about crying over a lost generation? How about crying over the homeless, the addicted, and the needy? How about crying over the devastating effects of sin, and the degradation of our youth?

One day in the late 1950s, David Wilkerson opened a copy of *Life* magazine, where he saw photos of young gang members in New York City. Looking into their eyes, he broke down and wept. This young pastor left the shelter of his country church to bring the gospel to the toughest gangs in New York City. He went *"out weeping, carrying seed to sow,"* and yes, David Wilkerson returned *"with songs of joy, carrying sheaves with him."* He proved that the message of the cross is more powerful than the switchblade.

God has given us His seed—the Word of God—for a reason. We are to scatter it out in the world. There can be no harvest unless someone goes out and plants the seed.

Are you carrying seed to sow? Don't just carry it into the world. Scatter it. There is no joy quite like the harvester's joy. The harvester has worked with God, and the LORD's joy becomes his own.

"He who goes out weeping, carrying seed to sow, will return with songs of joy, carrying sheaves with him."

Bringing Life to the Psalms

1. Have you experienced the joy of harvest, where new souls have been added to the Kingdom of God? What was that experience like? What role did you play? Read 1 Corinthians 3:5–9 for Paul's perspective on planting and harvesting.

2. What is the difference between ingathering and revival? There appears to be a place for both in the economy of God's Kingdom.

Take note of the revival that took place under the leadership of Josiah, King of Judah, recorded in 2 Chronicles 34–35. The discovery of the Book of the Law of the LORD was a key element in this revival. In a similar way, I would contend that the release of the *Good News New Testament* by the Bible Society contributed significantly to the Jesus People movement of the early 1970s. How important is it for you to have an understandable translation of the Scriptures?

3. Are we living in a harsh spiritual climate? Is the gospel message impacting the culture in which we live, or is the culture of the world impacting the church?

4. What are you personally doing to sow the seed of God's Word? What are some innovative ways to get the seed out into the field? What can churches do to facilitate going out with the seed of God's Word? Have you circled the wagons? Are you merely entertaining yourself? What is the role of tears in the harvest that God wills to bring on the earth?

5. Reread Psalm 126. What is God saying to you by His Spirit?

Full Redemption

A Song of ascents.

Out of the depths I cry out to you, O LORD;
    O LORD, hear my voice.
Let your ears be attentive
    to my cry for mercy.
If you, O LORD, kept a record of sins,
    O LORD, who could stand?
But with you there is forgiveness;
    therefore you are feared.

I wait for the LORD, my soul waits,
    and in his word I put my hope.
My soul waits for the LORD
more than watchmen wait for the morning,
more than watchmen wait for the morning.

O Israel, put your hope in the LORD,
    for with the LORD is unfailing love
    and with him is full redemption.
He himself will redeem Israel
    from all their sins.

I HAVE A SECRET TO SHARE. One of the reasons I love the Psalms so much is because, by reading them, I can become a spiritual voyeur. The Psalms let me see what most people hide. They take me gently by the hand and lead me into the inner sanctum of the human soul. Here I see men in travail with their God. Here I see the ecstasy of worship—joyous and unrestrained. Here I see everything laid bare before the One who sees all. Here I discover what it means to know God and be fully known by Him.

I come away saying, "So this is what loving God looks like. So this is what it means to be in a soul-bonding relationship with the Maker of the universe."

In the Psalms we catch a glimpse of intimate times with God, and we discover how these times can become our own. This is the Bible's explicit *How-to Manual for Intimacy with God.*

Psalm 130 is a perfect example of a psalm that brings us into the private inner sanctum of communion with God. Here is a portrait of a fallen man—a man on his knees before his Maker, the eternal One. Hear him now as he agonizes in prayer, "*Out of the depths I cry out to you, O LORD; O LORD, hear my voice. Let your ears be attentive to my cry for mercy.*"

The opening lines of this psalm leave little doubt as to what has transpired. The psalmist has failed; he has missed the mark. He has transgressed yet again. There is an abject poverty of spirit reflected in these words—a poverty that almost makes us cringe.

We do not know what sin, or list of sins, has brought the psalmist to this wretched state. The transgression is left unstated. Was it anger, malice, or unbridled lust? Was it pride, greed, or willful dishonesty? Was this a transgression of the mind, of the tongue, of action or inaction? Or was it some combination or permutation of all of these? God knows. We are left guessing.

But a forthright appraisal of my own soul leaves ample latitude for the scope and the severity of sin. I am always somewhat skeptical of those who sanctimoniously claim they could never commit this sin or that sin. I think we rarely comprehend the depravity of our own hearts. If pushed into wrong circumstances, in the wrong environment, with the wrong peer group, who can plumb the depths to which a man or woman may sink?

I am human, tainted by the fall, the original transgression. I can identify with the psalmist. I have added my own pile of dung to this world's heap of moral filth. I too have found myself in the psalmist's position, sobbing out these words, *"Out of the depths I cry out to you, O LORD; O LORD, hear my voice. Let your ears be attentive to my cry for mercy."*

But … despite my failings, despite my moral poverty, this great God—this God of holiness—is approachable. He is a God of mercy. The psalmist reminds himself and the LORD of His merciful nature.

"If you, O LORD, kept a record of sins, O LORD, who could stand? But with you there is forgiveness; therefore you are feared."

I need daily reminders of the mercy of God. God the moral accountant is also the LORD of forgiveness. No one does forgiveness better than God. He destroys the record. What accountant does that?

It is income tax time right now as I complete this manuscript, so I find myself caught between completing this book and completing my tax return. My accountant always insists that I keep all my receipts, all my records, and every slip of paper. He warns that at some point in the future, the revenue department may decide to do an audit of my tax account.

But with God there is no future audit. Every sin I have brought to Him has been erased. It's been destroyed. The LORD has no record of it. He can't find it, and He's not even looking for it. It's gone. Gone forever!

Wow! What an amazing God! He makes sins disappear. He keeps no records. He is a forgiving God; hence He is feared. The psalmist clearly states, *"But with you there is forgiveness; therefore you are feared."*

Now that is a rather curious statement. The forgiveness of God produces in us a reverent fear of the Great Forgiver. We respect, honor, and worship the LORD because He forgives—not because He mocks us for our errors and slams us into the jail cell of guilt. No, just the opposite is true. God forgives—not once or twice, but repeatedly. He forgives on day one thousand just as freely as He did on day one. He has no remembrance of our first offence. He has no record of it. A purposeful, divine senility has set in. Yet the Ancient of Days is still omniscient; He knows everything. He chooses to forgive me and to see me as faultless. I have an unblemished record because there is no record of my wrongs.

Because He forgives, I love Him. Because He forgives, I fear Him, and I will serve Him all the days of my life. He is a shelter for the fallen. He is help for the failing. He is an anchor for the wayward. When I cry out from the depths, He hears. The LORD is there.

And He is here now. He listens. He is listening to our thoughts. His Holy Spirit convicts us of sin and then wrenches us into alignment with the Almighty. Yes, the gentle Holy Spirit forces us into soul-altering repentance. By forcing us, I mean the Spirit works on our stubborn, hell-bent will until we yield to the will of God. This is the soul-wrenching experience of every God-encountering believer, and we are witnessing such an encounter here within this psalm.

Psalm 130 can be divided into three distinct sections: the confessional approach, the wait, and the LORD's response. Thus far, we have been looking at the confessional approach. The psalmist comes before his God and pours out his heart. In desperation he pleads for mercy and forgiveness. At the same time, he acknowledges the extreme mercy of God. He knows full well that this God forgives the undeserving.

Now the psalmist waits.

"I wait for the LORD, my soul waits, and in his word I put my hope. My soul waits for the LORD more than watchmen wait for the morning, more than watchmen wait for the morning."

This is the step that is most frequently missing in our communion with God. We cannot wait. We rush on. We have things to do, people to see, a life to live. We have no time to wait for the LORD's response.

But without waiting, we cannot hear the LORD speaking to our hearts. The rush of life takes over. We do not hear Him speak the words of divine pardon. We do not hear the voice of our Savior. Prayer is reduced to one-way communication. We speak into the silence and allow no time for the God of silence to answer back. By our actions we insist that God must respect our timetable.

How many times has the LORD tried to call you, and all He has heard from your end of the line is an annoying busy signal? Will our merciful God continue to call?

What a different response we see from the psalmist. "*I wait for the LORD, my soul waits, and in his word I put my hope. My soul waits for the LORD more than watchmen wait for the morning, more than watchmen wait for the morning.*"

The repetition of that last line adds a certain gravity to every word. There is resolute determination in these words. I can hear the psalmist saying to himself, "I'm not going anywhere until the LORD answers. I need to hear His voice for myself. I need to hear the pardon from His lips."

In this time of waiting, the psalmist turns to the written word of God. He states, "*In his word I put my hope.*"

Where do you turn as you wait for God to answer your prayers?

Turn to God's Word. Read it. Meditate on it. Let it fill your soul. From the pages of His Word, God speaks. Put your hope in God's enduring Word.

Next we encounter the third transition within the poetic structure of Psalm 130. There is a one-line break and then the psalmist continues. There is a dramatic change from this point on. Here is the third section—the LORD's response. The psalmist is no longer addressing the LORD in humble prayer. Now he is addressing us. It is as though the psalmist has heard from God within that blank line on the page. The waiting is over. God has spoken and now the psalmist rises to his feet. He has a message from the LORD for us, the Israel of God.

"O Israel, put your hope in the LORD, for with the LORD is unfailing love and with him is full redemption."

For Israel, there was a long wait. The promised Messiah was a long time in coming. The centuries slipped by. Generation after generation passed on, but the Word of the LORD stood firm. A redeemer was coming. The ongoing question remained, "Will He come in my day? Will I see His face?"

With uncanny accuracy, the Old Testament prophets foretold the coming of the Christ. Many of those prophesies are found within the book of Psalms. In Psalm 22, with agonizing detail, David portrayed Christ's suffering on the cross. Jesus Himself drew attention to this prophetic link, as He cried out from the cross, *"My God, my God, why have you forsaken me?"* (Psalm 22:1; Matthew 27:46).

Now speaking with personal assurance that his sins are forgiven, the psalmist declares, *"O Israel, put your hope in the LORD, for with the LORD is unfailing love and with him is full redemption."*

The LORD is our fount of hope. He is love and the source of unfailing love. It is He who will redeem us body, soul, and spirit.

"He himself will redeem Israel from all their sins."

This is not a job for sacrificial lambs and goats or the ashes of a heifer. The LORD *"himself will redeem Israel from all their sins."*

What a revelation! Redemption in the old covenant involved the shedding of blood. From the time of the first Passover, the firstborn of Israel belonged to the LORD. They were to be redeemed by an animal sacrifice. But here, through the voice of the psalmist, the LORD makes clear that the old sacrificial system will be superseded. *"He himself will redeem Israel from all their sins."*

The God of heaven will come in person—He, Himself. He will come in human form and stretch out His hands to draw all humanity to Himself—every infant, every girl and boy, every woman and man—all are included. He will Himself redeem us from our sins. He will take the spikes on our behalf, in our stead. He will bleed for us. The remedy for sin will be found at the foot of the cross.

The psalmist's closing words echo Abraham's words on the way to Mount Moriah, the hill of sacrifice. Abraham told Isaac, *"God himself will provide the lamb for the burnt offering, my son"* (Genesis 22:8).

God Himself will provide. He will provide Himself. He will provide *"the Lamb of God, who takes away the sin of the world"* (John 1:29).

So through the Psalms, this spiritual voyeur is brought from beneath the starry hosts to the most intimate place—the place of the cross. There, water and blood flow mingling down. Filthy and naked I come, and there I am washed clean—clean by the blood of the Lamb.

Bringing Life to the Psalms

1. In what respect are the Psalms a *How-to Manuel for Intimacy with God?* Do you agree or disagree with this description?

2. Take time to consider the three sections of this psalm: the confessional approach, the wait, and the LORD's response. Can this become a pattern for your own times of prayer?

3. There is a prophetic element to this psalm. Where does that prophetic element come from? Does it come from waiting on God? Read Psalm 22 and reflect on the revelation given to David in that psalm.

4. Take time to read Genesis 22. Read it from a father's perspective. Then read it from Isaac's perspective. Finally, try to view this account from our heavenly Father's perspective. What do you believe was God's intent in all of this?

5. Rejoice! The LORD Himself has stretched out His hands and redeemed you from all your sins!

Epilogue

For almost ten years now, I have been doing dramatic performances of the fourteen psalms covered in this book at church services and events in Canada and the United States. Yes, as an actor, I have been performing the Psalms.

It's wonderful to see the effect the dramatized Psalms have upon an audience. The Psalms are so intimate—at times uncomfortably so. I meet with God in the Psalms, and one can sense His presence as His word is brought to life. We are face to face and, as the drama of the moment unfolds, a hushed silence fills the sanctuary.

God is with us.

He is here.

He indwells His Word.

The heartbreaking confession, the blest ecstasy of worship, the silent communion—all are portrayed within the Psalms. In my performance, my goal is to bring all present to Throne of Grace, to the place of transformation. My unspoken prayer is, "Come now, Holy Spirit. Come!"

Thankfully, He does come. He honors the Word of God. The Word springs to life. It leaps off the pages of the Bible and dances into the hearts of those who hear it. It needs no further explanation. It is powerful of its own accord. It is God-breathed and alive!

I catch glimpses of the results later as people testify. The most common response is, "You brought the Psalms alive! I see them in a whole new light. Now I want to dig into God's Word."

"You brought the Psalms alive!"

Of course, the Psalms have always been alive. They have never ceased living and working in the hearts of those who read and apply them, and for me that is the most encouraging truth about the Psalms. They come to life. They come to live within us. The Psalms have come to my life and they are doing a transformational work.

I publicly perform the Psalms, but privately the Psalms have been performing a work within me. Public performance has meant that I must memorize the Psalms, and from time to time rehearse them in my mind to keep them fresh. What an exercise that has been! My prayer life has been invigorated. My worship times have been infused with joy. Now through practical application, I understand the principle of incorporating the Word of God.

We all understand the principle of incorporation when it comes to the food we eat. The food we eat becomes the body we live in and provides the energy that drives our life forward. Of course, what is true of the natural body is also true of human spirit. If we read, memorize, and digest the Word of God, it becomes life to us. We live on its energy—an energy that comes from the God who is the source of all life.

Wow! The Word of God is performing in me. Since I began performing the Psalms, more than ever before I can say, "The Word of God is transforming my relationships and my life into the likeness of Jesus."

The Word is alive and when it is digested it becomes our life—a life sourced not in the world or in self, but rather a life sourced in God. The Word always seeks to become incarnate. It must be lived. My prayer is that through applying the Psalms, the Word may take form within you.

Each of my "Psalms Alive!" performances ends with Psalm 130 and a portrayal of Christ's sacrificial death on the cross. When we come face to face with God, we see Jesus. He is the LORD of the Psalms. The lover of my soul transforms me by His love. Seeing Him changes my life.

May it change your life as well.

> *Whenever anyone turns to the Lord, the veil is taken away. Now the Lord is the Spirit, and where the Spirit of the Lord is, there is freedom. And we, who with unveiled faces all reflect the LORD's glory, are being transformed into his likeness with ever-increasing glory, which comes from the Lord, who is the Spirit* (2 Corinthians 3:16–18).

I pray that the Psalms may perform their work in you as well.
May you live in the Word.
May you live by the Word.
May you live through the indwelling Spirit-power of the Word.

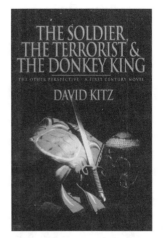